INSTRUCTOR'S MANUAL FOR
CASE STUDIES ON
EDUCATIONAL
ADMINISTRATION

INSTRUCTOR'S MANUAL FOR
CASE STUDIES ON EDUCATIONAL ADMINISTRATION

Theodore J. Kowalski

Teachers College
Ball State University

Longman
New York & London

Instructor's Manual for Case Studies on Educational Administration

Longman, 95 Church Street, White Plains, N.Y. 10601

Associated companies:
Longman Group Ltd., London
Longman Cheshire Pty., Melbourne
Longman Paul Pty., Auckland
Copp Clark Pitman, Toronto

ISBN: 0-8013-0388-5

ABCDEFGHIJ-VG-99 98 97 96 95 94 93 92 91 90

INSTRUCTOR'S MANUAL FOR CASE STUDIES ON EDUCATIONAL ADMINISTRATION

Introduction
CASE 1: The Principal Changes Some Valued Rules   1
CASE 2: Management Is Management: Or Is It?   11
CASE 3: Setting Higher Standards   20
CASE 4: Too Many Schools   28
CASE 5: An Assistant Principal Who Does Not
          Fit the Image   36
CASE 6: Program Expansion or Budget Cuts?   44
CASE 7: Using Committees to Make Key Decisions   53
CASE 8: An Effort to Study School-Based Management   60
CASE 9: Involving Teachers in Employment Decisions   69
CASE 10: Restricting Employment Opportunities   77
CASE 11: The Closed Door Policy   84
CASE 12: Captain Punishment   90
CASE 13: The Stepping Stone   96
CASE 14: Success Is Spelled "PR, PR, PR"   102
CASE 15: Sorcerer Will Help You Spell It   108
CASE 16: Whose Philosophy Will Control
          Collective Bargaining?   114
CASE 17: Who Will Censure This Board Member?   126
CASE 18: Differing Perceptions of Teaching
          Effectiveness   131
CASE 19: Trying to Prevent Unionization   138
CASE 20: Let's Not Rap   145
CASE 21: Who Decides Standards for Employing
          a Principal?   150
CASE 22: "Narc" or Social Worker? or Maybe
          Educational Leader?   156
CASE 23: Never, Never, Never Try to Get in the
          Taxpayer's Pocket   163
CASE 24: The Clinic Controversy   169
CASE 25: A Matter of Honor   175
Reading List for Case Method   183

INTRODUCTION

Three points of information will be helpful in using this instructor's manual. The first relates to the organization of the twenty-five cases in the book; the second concerns the internal organization of the individual cases; and the third explains the general purpose of <u>Case Studies on Educational Administration</u>. Please read this section carefully before proceeding.

ORGANIZATION OF THE CASES WITHIN THE BOOK

Most student textbooks are written in chronological form. That is, the material is presented sequentially. For example, that which appears in the second chapter is often an extension of what appears in the first chapter. <u>Case Studies on Educational Administration</u> does not follow this type of format. After the introductory section, the twenty-five cases are presented without any deliberate pattern of topics or concepts. As the book is used in a variety of graduate courses and seminars, it was decided not to group or intentionally sequence the cases.

For your convenience, a matrix identifying primary themes for the twenty-five cases is provided in the introductory materials. The following information relates to using this matrix:

1. Because the twenty-five cases are not presented in any specified order, the matrix permits you to select those cases that have relevance to your instructional objectives.

2. Each case has more than one focus. For example, a case may relate to organizational theory as well as career development. In some instances the cases may have as many as five or six foci.

3. The foci identified in the matrix merely provide suggested areas of emphasis. As you become more familiar with the cases you may well identify additional topics that can evolve from the situations presented.

MATRIX FOR IDENTIFYING PRIMARY THEMES

(Case Number)

	1	2	3	4	5	6	7	8	9	10	11	12	13	14	15	16	17	18	19	20	21	22	23	24	25
ADMINISTRATIVE POSITION																									
Superintendent										x	x	x	x	x	x	x	x	x	x	x	x		x	x	x
Asst. Superintendent	x		x		x	x	x	x	x		x			x	x	x						x	x	x	
High School Principal					x	x		x	x				x							x		x			x
Middle School Principal						x		x	x			x							x						
Elementary School Principal	x																								
Assistant Principal				x					x			x			x			x	x			x			
Other Central Office		x									x					x							x		
LEVEL OF SCHOOL																									
School District		x	x	x			x		x	x	x		x	x	x	x	x	x		x	x		x		
High School					x	x			x								x	x	x		x	x		x	x
Middle School						x						x												x	
Elementary School	x														x	x	x	x	x	x					x
LOCATION																									
Rural									x	x						x	x							x	
Suburban		x		x							x				x				x			x		x	
Urban/Large City	x		x									x		x							x		x		x
Town/Small City		x			x	x	x	x					x					x		x					

ADMINISTRATIVE AREAS

	1	2	3	4	5	6	7	8	9	10	11	12	13	14	15	16	17	18	19	20	21	22	23	24	25	26	27	28	29
Collective Bargaining		x								x							x							x				
Community Relations	x	x		x		x					x	x		x	x				x		x		x	x	x	x	x	
Curriculum & Instruction			x	x		x					x				x			x						x				x
Evaluation			x		x	x			x				x		x			x					x					
Finance		x		x		x	x								x										x			
Leadership Behavior	x			x	x	x	x	x	x		x	x	x	x	x	x		x	x	x			x	x	x	x		
Legal Issues						x						x													x			
Personnel		x			x				x	x			x			x		x	x		x							
Policy Development	x	x	x	x		x	x	x		x		x			x	x			x		x	x	x		x	x		

CONTEMPORARY ISSUES

	1	2	3	4	5	6	7	8	9	10	11	12	13	14	15	16	17	18	19	20	21	22	23	24	25	26	27	28	29
Communication Problems	x		x		x	x		x	x	x	x		x	x		x			x		x							
Collaborative Decisions						x	x	x	x					x										x				
Decisions & Conflict	x	x			x	x	x	x	x			x		x		x			x		x			x	x			
Declining Enrollments		x		x																	x		x	x				
Discipline	x									x											x		x	x				
Educational Reform Efforts		x					x								x													
Ethical Issues		x		x		x		x					x	x	x				x		x						x	
Multicultural Education	x		x				x		x					x		x		x		x		x	x					
Parental Conflict	x		x				x			x			x	x	x		x					x	x					
School Board Relations		x	x			x		x			x	x		x		x		x			x							
Teachers				x		x	x			x			x		x			x										
Women Administrators			x	x	x		x		x		x	x	x	x	x	x		x		x								

4. To use the matrix, find the area(s) of emphasis you desire in the first column. By going across the row, the X's identify the cases that contain material for the focus.

5. This matrix does not appear in the student text; however, a subject index is provided in that book.

ORGANIZATION OF INDIVIDUAL CASES

You will note that the format for the narrative portions of the twenty-five cases varies. Some cases are purposefully divided into pieces of information. For example, the community, school district, and school are described in separate sections of the case. Other cases are presented without subheadings. With regard to the format for individual cases, please note the following:

1. Although it would have been more convenient to provide a standardized format for each of the twenty-five cases, this notion was rejected. The primary reason for varying format is quite simple. In real life, administrators do not receive information in neat, standardized packages. Often the practitioner must search for pertinent data and facts. Thus, the differing formats for the narrative portions of the cases serve to nurture the student's ability to work with varying structures of information.

2. Although the narrative portions are not uniform, the remainder of case presentations are consistent (i.e., Challenge, Key Issues/Questions, and Suggested Readings).

GENERAL PURPOSE OF *CASE STUDIES ON EDUCATIONAL ADMINISTRATION*

The text is designed to be a vehicle for permitting students to apply acquired knowledge and skills, and to do so in a reflective manner. A myriad of instructional purposes can be achieved through the case method of teaching: developing contingencies, examining the effects of environment on instructional decisions, reinforcing acquired knowledge, and so forth.

One of the critical choices you must make relates to your overall purpose in using the cases. Masoner (1988) described this choice as one between induction and application. If you are teaching new concepts, then the cases are used to promote induction. If you are using the cases to see if students can apply concepts already covered in previous courses or lessons, then the cases are used for application. In business courses the predominant use has been in application. Although the cases in this book could be used for teaching new concepts, they were selected more for application activities. Some universities offer a simulations course for students pursuing certification as administrators. This text is especially useful in this type of experience. The most common use, however, is to inject cases into the content of basic courses in educational administration (e.g., organizational theory, personnel administration, the principalship).

INTRODUCTION TO USING THE CASE STUDY METHOD

Many textbooks provide some case studies, but few are devoted entirely to this form of study. By far the most recognized achievements in the use of the case method for teaching belong to the Harvard Business School faculty. Ever since the early part of this century, the Harvard faculty has used case studies to expose students to real situations in the business world. The continued emphasis on case studies is evidenced by the recent edition of Teaching and the Case Method (Christensen, 1987) published by the Harvard Business School.

The use of cases in education texts is usually limited to supplemental activities. As such, there is little or no explanation of the potentialities of case studies as an instructional tool. This introductory section defines the case study method, examines the possible benefits related to its use, examines criticisms, and provides a framework for using the instructor's manual.

DEFINING THE CASE STUDY METHOD

Frequently, the terms case study and case method are used interchangeably. This is confusing. Case study usually refers to a broad process that may have several different purposes: (1) as a method of <u>research</u>, (2) as a method of <u>evaluation</u>, (3) as a method of <u>policy studies</u>, and (4) as a <u>teaching method</u>. For this reason, it is essential to define three related terms:

Case work: the development, adjustment, remedial, or corrective procedures that appropriately follow diagnosis of the causes of maladjustment. Case work is a common term in psychology, sociology, social work, and medicine.

Case method: an instructional technique whereby the major ingredients of a case study are presented to students for the purpose of studying potential behaviors or in problem solving.

Case history: tracing a person, group, or organization's past (Merriam, 1988). Dooley and Skinner (1977) contended that the term <u>case method</u> embraces so many pedagogical practices that the term itself has no precise meaning. Nevertheless, case method commonly refers to the use of case studies, or elements thereof, for instructional purposes. The case is used to generate reactions and discussions.

A variety of definitions are offered for the term <u>case study</u>. Some writers focus on the research aspect (Yin, 1984), some focus on the differences between analytical and descriptive studies (Shaw, 1978), and still others focus on social structure (Becker, 1968). Foreman (1948) offered the following definition: **A case study, basically, is a depiction either of a phase or the totality of relevant experience of some selected datum** (p. 408). In general, there is no one universally accepted definition of case study (Oldham & Forrester, 1981). This fact needs to be emphasized to students. Often individuals believe that case studies must conform to prescribed standards in order to be correctly labeled case studies. Although uniformity may be observed in certain medical fields (e.g., the case history), this is not true of case studies in general.

Some characteristics of the case study are noteworthy. In her analysis of the use of case studies in adult education research, Merriam (1988) identified the following attributes:

1. Case studies usually relate to qualitative research and naturalistic inquiry. Such studies are often referred to as ethnographic study, field study, or participant observations.

2. Data in case studies are collected by observation, interview, or document analysis.

3. Case studies use logical rather than statistical bases for generalizations.

4. There is little consensus among users of case studies as to how to deal with the questions of validity, reliability, and generalizability.

5. Guidelines for actually writing case studies--that is, length, style, ethics--are not well-developed in the literature.

For purposes here, it is important to note that the term <u>case study</u> is a comprehensive way of referring to the entire process of collecting and reporting data. <u>Case method</u> refers to use of case studies for instructional purposes. Cases commonly fall into one of three categories: (1) true cases, (2) disguised cases, or (3) fictitious cases (Matejka & Cosse, 1981). Fictitious cases are also referred to as <u>armchair cases.</u> In the first category, no data of any type are changed. In the second, the facts remain intact, but the names of actors, locations, organizations, and the like are altered to assure anonymity. The third category utilizes hypothetical examples to illustrate a principle, concept, or specific set of conditions.

USE OF THE CASE STUDY METHOD

The case study is advocated as one alternative for infusing reality into the academic preparation of educational leaders. The need to explore actual problems and challenges is reinforced by various national reports such as <u>A Nation Prepared</u> (Task Force on Teaching as a Profession, 1986). Schools are complex organizations, so study of the administrator's work environment is enhanced when cases focusing on common conditions are used as an instructional tool. Unlike most other organizations, the school is concerned with human, not material, products. This fact introduces unique problems for professional employees. The work-day of administrators is tremendously intricate. Virtually all administrative behavior can be viewed as a mix of economic, political, social, psychological, and managerial factors.

Using the case study method can produce many positive outcomes. Consider some of the more obvious benefits of using cases as a teaching tool:

1. Cases provide an excellent format for the development of critical-thinking skills. Students are encouraged to analyze their own behavior as well as the behavior of others. The case method allows reflection, an element missing in the traditional lecture/reading methods of teaching.

2. Cases provide an excellent format for developing problem-solving skills. Students learn to identify and analyze contingencies, to develop alternative courses of action, and to make decisions.

3. Cases provide a process of participatory learning. Unlike the lecture method where students are passive participants, the case method actively engages the student in discussion with the professor and other students.

4. Cases require students to perform. Acquired knowledge is used to analyze environmental conditions and to make decisions. The case method is an <u>active</u> process focusing on decisions.

5. Cases expose students to the complexities of organizational life. Schools are multifaceted organizations composed of individuals and groups. Encountering problems in the context of differing environments allows students to view the varying organizational climates of schools.

6. Cases permit students to discuss and debate selected courses of action. Many of the qualities of interactive learning are automatically incorporated into the case method. Administrators need to acquire the skills necessary for formulating numerous acceptable and wise decisions.

7. Cases help students make mature judgments about extremely complex problems. By seeing how others react to the same problem, students are better able to analyze a range of available alternatives. They have opportunities to gain insight into the factors that motivate individuals to specific courses of action.

The issue of self-study in relation to administrative practice is critical to the case method of teaching. Schon (1984) offered the following observation:

Reflective managers continually interrogate their ways of framing their roles and their problematic situations, the way in which they build and use their repertoires of images and exemplars, the models of the world which underlie their behavior, the processes by which they shape and interpret experiments, and the ways in which their private inquiries interact with the learning system of the organization of which they are members. (p. 62)

The major purpose of reflective practice is the development of augmented professional intelligence--using theory not directly in practice but rather as a tool to inform practice (Sergiovanni, 1987). That is, the administrator learns to integrate knowledge with experience and to recognize that all experiences and challenges are somewhat novel.

In large measure, the ultimate value of the case method is embodied in the belief that decisions regarding serious matters transcend specified techniques (Plante, 1987). Behavior that succeeds in one situation may fail in another. A myriad of environmental conditions converge to create a unique footing for each case. The technique of the case method offers students an opportunity to understand why "successful" practice, at least in part, depends on the environment and specific organizational conditions at the particular time. For this reason, general and specific problem-solving skills are deemed important. General skills provide a framework applicable to all situations. Specific skills permit general knowledge to be fused with data and conditions specific to a given situation.

There are two universal facets of the case method. First, this paradigm entails the Socratic Method. Second, cases always provide what is labeled situational knowledge. Situational knowledge includes the facts and information the student receives from reading the case study (Masoner, 1988). This information is uniform because all students read the same cases. Why then do students often arrive at different interpretations and conclusions?

When students absorb specific knowledge they process this information through abstractions. Concepts, values, experiences, and beliefs held by the students are not identical. When they formulate abstractions using situational knowledge, they develop varying forms of specific knowledge, that is, the knowledge base created after the process of abstraction. Another way to look at this is to consider

xv

situational knowledge as the input, abstraction as the processing element, and specific knowledge as the output.

Successful implementation requires planning. In reviewing the literature on the case method Romm & Mahler (1986) concluded that three factors are related to positive outcome: (1) a careful choice of interesting, thought provoking cases by the instructor; (2) an in-depth preparation of the case by the instructor and students prior to class discussion; and, (3) flexibility and openness on the part of both the instructor and students during the analysis phase.

Goals for the case method can be divided into two distinct categories: (1) the objective domain, and (2) the affective domain. Examples of potential goals in the objective domain are:
* reasoning
* creativity
* critical thinking
* integration and decision making
* general problem-solving skills
* specific knowledge problem-solving skills
* gaining knowledge via induction
* application of knowledge learned by initial coverage
Examples of goals in the affective domain are:
* confidence
* working with others
* professional responsibility
* empathy

One of the most common purposes of using the case method is to develop reasoning skills in leaders. This can take place in four distinct contexts: (1) the direct induction of specific concepts from situational knowledge; (2) the integration of evidence; (3) the integration of arguments (i.e., integrating diverse opinions); and, (4) the integration of various perspectives (e.g., the ability to see a problem from someone else's perspective).

Regardless of purpose, it is critically important for you to determine your goals prior to using the case method. Criticism of this teaching paradigm often stems from situations where instructors rely on serendipity for positive results. Your instructional goals ought to determine the way you use cases.

USING THE CASE METHOD

A primary concern in the use of the case method is the determination of exactly how students will become involved in the process. Three critically important factors are considered in making this decision, as illustrated by the following questions:

1. What is your style of teaching? Are you willing to allocate sufficient time for the use of cases?

2. What will be the levels of involvement for the students? Will each student be expected to address each case? Will there be varying roles for the students?

3. What discussion techniques will be used to analyze responses to the cases? Will you permit a free exchange between the students? For example, you may decide to be very nondirective and allow students to react freely to the cases. Or, you may decide to be highly directive, specifying precisely what you expect of each student as the cases are used in class (Dooley & Skinner, 1977).

Most often, the instructor assumes the role of discussion leader. This can be a complicated task. Some cases may ignite instant discussion, whereas others may require the instructor to use stimuli. Knowing when to interrupt a student discussion is critically important. You will want to strike a careful balance between encouraging creativity and preventing one or two students from dominating discussion. One way to accomplish this is by carefully questioning the students. This assures greater participation levels by all. Discussion is a valuable instructional tool because students learn both from their own analyses and from peer reactions. Teaching with cases produces a form of cooperative learning.

Even where instructional goals are carefully planned and articulated, the case method may produce some unexpected outcomes. For example, a student's reaction to a particular case may illuminate some facet of the administrator's role that is not perceived by others. That is, the reaction may present a novel perception regarding one of the characters in the case. In these instances you should be flexible and pursue the student's interests, curiosity, or concern.

Before initiating the case method, you may wish to discuss the purposes of this instructional technique with your students. As with all other methods of teaching, students should know the goals and objectives of the activity. A written explanation of the case method provides a reference for the learner.

The cases in the text are purposefully not taken to their conclusion. Consequently you can use simulation techniques in conjunction with the cases. This text was designed to allow significant instructor self-determination.

You decide the context in which the cases will be used (e.g., simulation, group discussion), and you determine the nature and level of your own involvement. In some instances, the text may serve as the primary guide for a course; in other situations it may be used as a supplemental text. The following are some of the more common strategies for teaching with cases:

1. Identify one student to react to the case and have other students analyze the response(s).

2. Select several, but not all, students to respond to a case. Those not selected for this task are assigned the responsibility of reacting/evaluating peer responses.

3. Provide all students the case as an out-of-class assignment. When completed, the products are shared and analyzed in class.

4. When time permits, use role-playing as a means for presenting cases. Selected students are instructed to react in specific ways to cases and other students evaluate the behavior. You can predetermine a range of behaviors, which is a distinct advantage.

5. Form discussion groups to react to the cases. That is, have a small group of students collectively decide on a course of action. After decisions are reached, the group can share and discuss its responses with the remainder of the class.

6. You may wish to build a lecture around a case. For example, you could predetermine possible behaviors and then offer an analysis for each alternative. This application obviously diminishes the interactive potentialities of using cases, but it may be suitable for very large classes.

You may prefer to alter discussion methods regardless of the specific technique you are using. If only discussion groups are used in case analysis, insight into individual abilities may never be attained. For this reason, it is occasionally advisable to assign students independent work related to the cases.

Students relate cases to real situations with which they are familiar. Where this occurs you should direct the conversation away from personal attacks on individuals or organizations. The case method can evolve into discussions inappropriate for the college classroom unless proper supervision is exercised.

Another discussion opportunity involves inviting resource persons into the class to participate in the analysis of specific cases (e.g., a lawyer is invited to react to cases focusing on legal issues). This procedure is especially useful if cases involve practitioners in other professions.

It is important that the instructor create an environment where students feel free to interact. Care must be taken to dissuade students from unduly criticizing or ridiculing peer responses. Occasionally, it will be necessary for the instructor to intervene when unworkable or unacceptable responses are provided (e.g., when a student selects a course of action that is clearly illegal) or when some students become too critical or abusive of peer responses. If students are allowed to attack each other, some will become fearful of the process and withdraw.

In preparing for the first class, it is helpful to select reactors carefully. Students with more extroverted personalities and self-confidence may perform better in the initial case experience. Some students will have tremendous difficulty making a decision, whereas others will be ready to pick an immediate course of action. Some students are risk takers, others are not. Fear of failure is another important consideration in selecting the students. For these reasons, you may wish to get to know your students before making case assignments.

A major purpose of using cases in educational administration is to integrate theory to a given situation. Your task as the professor is to provide guidance in creating these linkages. As you prepare to use cases, it is advisable to outline theories relevant to the situation.

A summation activity for each case is recommended. That is, the instructor should provide some assessment and comment before the class moves on to other material. This assessment will depend on the types of discussion and analysis used; however, in all instances it should provide a summary of the key issues and the relevant responses elicited via the discussions. This type of capstone experience is especially needed when divergent responses are given.

In this manual you will find the following information related to each case:

1. background information identifying the primary foci of each case;

2. some reactions to questions presented in the student text;

3. either suggested topics for further discussion or alternative questions to raise based on potential student responses; and

4. Suggested Readings.

The Suggested Readings presented in this manual are somewhat more extensive than those listed in the text. This will permit you to consider the assignment of additional readings. Or, you may choose to use these additional readings to prepare your comments and directions for a given case. Several points of information about the cases should be noted:

1. Many of the readings come from major texts being used currently in courses in educational administration. Hopefully, your students will already have read some of these books.

2. The readings are purposefully balanced between research- and theory- based articles/books and more practical-oriented pieces (e.g., material from The School Administrator or the Executive Educator).

3. It is advisable for you to develop a supplemental list of readings reflecting the specific academic experiences and needs of students at your institution.

Finally, it should be noted that the cases were not designed to produce one right answer. In each and every case, several responses are possible. The value of the case method lies in getting students to analyze and control the factors that contribute to decisions affecting their personal behavior. Like the case method itself, this book is designed to teach students that, as professionals, they have a responsibility to make decisions. As with real case situations, many of the cases require the students to determine what information is needed and then identify the best sources to tap for this information.

SOME FINAL THOUGHTS BEFORE STARTING

If you desire to learn more about using cases as a teaching paradigm, several books are recommended. One is the Christensen book from Harvard. Three other books are *The Art of Case Analysis* by Ronstadt (1980), *Teaching with Cases* by Erskine, Leenders, and Mauffette-Leenders (1981), and *An Audit of the Case Study Method* by Masoner (1988). If you wish to read additional material on reflection-in-action, Schon's books, *The Reflective Practitioner* (1983) and *Educating the Reflective Practitioner* (1990) are recommended. Each is listed in the references following this introductory section.

The cases presented in the text are disguised, that is, the names of individuals, communities, and school districts have been changed. The cases were selected through interviews with a number of school administrators and through the author's own experiences as a practitioner, professor, and consultant. The cases were selected for a variety of reasons. Not all present catastrophic situations. But all do present situations representative of the challenges and problems that face contemporary practitioners.

Finally, you are encouraged to require students to maintain notebooks related to their experiences with the cases. Such a document provides a resource that many students claim to be helpful.

REFERENCES

Becker, H. (1968). Social observations and social case studies. *International encyclopedia of the social sciences*, Vol. 11, pp. 232-238. New York: Crowell, Collier & Macmillan.

Christensen, C. (1987). *Teaching and the case method*. Boston: Harvard Business School.

Dooley, A., & Skinner, W. (1977). Casing case method methods. *Academy of Management Review*, II, 277-289.

Erskine, J., Leenders, M., & Mauffette-Leenders, L. (1981). *Teaching with cases.* London, Canada: School of Business Administration, University of Western Ontario.

Foreman, P. (1948). The theory of case studies. *Social Forces,* 26(4), 408-419.

Masoner, M. (1988). *An audit of the case study method.* New York: Praeger.

Matejka, J., & Cosse, T. (1981). *The business case method: An introduction.* Richmond, VA: Robert F. Dame.

Merriam, S. (1988). *Case research in education.* San Francisco: Jossey-Bass.

Oldham, M., & Forrester, J. (1981). The use of case studies in pre-experience business education: Part I--the case method. *The Vocational Aspect of Education,* 33, 27-29.

Plante, P. (1987). *The art of decision making: Issues and cases in higher education.* New York: Macmillan.

Romm, T., & Mahler, S. (1986). A three dimensional model for using case studies in the academic classroom. *Higher Education,* 15, 677-696.

Ronstadt, R. (1980). *The art of case analysis.* Dover, MA: Lord Publishing.

Schon, D. (1983). *The reflective practitioner.* New York: Basic Books.

Schon, D. (1984). Leadership as reflection-in-action. In T. Sergiovanni & J.Corbally(Eds.),*Leadership and organizational culture*, pp.36-63. Urbana, IL: University of Illinois Press.

Schon, D. (1990). *Educating the reflective practitioner.* San Francisco: Jossey-Bass.

Sergiovanni, T. (1987). *The principalship: A reflective practice perspective.* Boston: Allyn & Bacon.

Shaw, K. (1978). Understanding the curriculum: The approach through case studies. *Curriculum Studies,* 10(1), 1-17.

Task Force on Teaching as a Profession. (1986). *A nation prepared: Teachers for the 21st century.* New York: Carnegie Forum.

Yin, R. (1984). *Case study research.* Beverly Hills, CA: Sage Publications.

THE PRINCIPAL CHANGES SOME VALUED RULES

BACKGROUND INFORMATION

Increasingly, inner-city schools are faced with opposing views regarding the scope of responsibility of public education for the total welfare of children. To some extent, this case falls within the parameters of this debate. The principal is convinced that the school must be an institution offering the child compassion and understanding. The teachers are concerned about student academic achievement and maintaining an orderly environment that permits them to devote their efforts to teaching. The case also focuses on decision making at the school level. The principal makes substantial changes in rules and regulations during the first two years of his assignment. Questions are raised regarding the association of the process to the outcome. That is, to what extent is teacher and parental dissatisfaction associated with the process that was used to implement change?

Another dimension of this case deals with a contemporary topic: at-risk students. In particular, the practice of retaining children at grade level is questioned. Although the information in the case clearly states that the principal is opposed to failing students, the reader is not provided with information regarding the motivation for this position. For example, does the principal oppose retentions because of his knowledge of research data or does he formulate his position solely on the basis of individual values and beliefs? This case has some similarities to Case 12. Both relate to discipline policies. Case 12 takes place at the middle school level and there are several environmental and organizational issues different from those in this case. In this case, it is the principal who objects to harsh discipline, whereas in Case 12, the situation is reversed. You may want to utilize Cases 1 and 12 in order because of their similarities.

THE CHALLENGE

In this case, the assistant superintendent already has offered one potential solution to the situation (giving the principal a job in her office). The key challenge associated with this case essentially requires two decisions: (1) Will the disposition of the principal be decided immediately? (2) What will be done with the principal? Research on leadership reveals that some individuals are inclined to make quick decisions, whereas others are prone to be cautious and seek additional information before acting. If students in your class exhibit differences with regard to this time dimension, it offers an excellent opportunity to inject this aspect of leadership behavior into the classroom discussion. Have your students reflect on this issue. Why are some individuals more inclined to act on impulse? Additional options available to the assistant superintendent are identified under Key Issues/Questions.

KEY ISSUES/QUESTIONS

1. *Identify the range of options available to the assistant superintendent in this matter.* The range of decisions that could be made is best analyzed by placing them into categories related to the decision on timing. For students who opt for an immediate action, the following courses of action may be cited:

a. Insist that the principal take the job in the central office, that is, make it an involuntary transfer.

b. Transfer the principal to another school as soon as a vacancy occurs.

c. Give the principal a choice of taking the position in the central office or taking an assignment as a classroom teacher.

d. Rule in favor of the principal, agreeing that he should have more time to test his beliefs about discipline.

e. Rule against the principal, concluding that he used poor judgment and ask for his resignation because he refused the offer to join the central administrative staff.

Students who elect to defer action may cite one of the following approaches:

a. Hold meetings with the teachers (and possibly parents) to attempt reconciliation in this matter.

b. Commission a study by impartial observers to determine if the teachers are justified in recommending the principal's removal.

c. Hold public hearings at the school that would permit

parents and teachers on both sides of this issue to state their views.

Regardless of the option selected, students should provide a complete justification for their leadership behavior. In particular, they should be able to evaluate the potential impact of their decision and to list the perceived advantages and disadvantages. Additionally, you may wish to ask the students if they can identify the factors influencing their decisions. For example, some students may cite knowing about an experience similar to the one presented in the case; some may refer to leadership theories; still others may describe the behavior of some administrator that is admired/respected.

2. *If you were the principal and wanted to change rules and regulations regarding discipline, would you have required consensus from the teachers to do so?* We know that some leaders are more democratic than others. What is of value here is to differentiate between principals who are consistently autocratic (because of personality or philosophy) and those who are selectively autocratic (based on the circumstances of a given situation). It is important to extract from students whether there are specific conditions associated with this case that lead them to either concur with or reject the principal's approach to changing rules and regulations. In other words, you should try to determine if students have attempted to analyze the conditions or are simply responding from a base of "feelings." Students opting for teacher consensus may provide three primary justifications: (1) philosophical (e.g., consensus is appropriate in a democratic society), (2) political (e.g., teachers will be more supportive of the outcomes if they participate in making the decisions), and (3) professional (e.g., teachers possess knowledge that will lead to a better decision and as professionals, they have a right to participate).

3. *Do you believe it was proper for Dr. Danton to offer the principal a job in central administration to resolve the issue? Why or why not?* One can only guess about the assistant superintendent's motivation in offering another job to the principal. Consider two rather different reasons: (1) The principal was considered very competent and the assistant superintendent would like to have him on her staff. This provides an excellent opportunity to achieve this goal and at the same time resolve a conflict. (2) The assistant

3

superintendent fears conflict and will do almost anything to eradicate it immediately. Judging Dr. Danton's behavior should be associated with potential motives. Students should be asked why they think Dr. Danton made this offer. This question also offers an opportunity to discuss bureaucratic theory in relation to conflict. If this were a highly closed organizational climate, pressure might be exerted to resolve conflict quickly, even if it meant accommodating those who generate the conflict.

4. *Is the principal correct in his judgment that corporal punishment and suspensions provide negative reinforcement that deters the development of self-discipline?* The debate regarding corporal punishment and other forms of punishment has three dimensions. One entails legal implications; a second focuses on behavioral studies (e.g., as in educational psychology); and the third relates to philosophy. Students should be able to discuss all three dimensions. In particular, students should become aware that there are different theories regarding student discipline and they should know where to access this information.

5. *Discuss the rights of the troubled child in relation to classmates. Are the teachers correct in their contention that permitting a disruptive child to remain in the classroom deprives other students of their opportunity to learn?* This issue divides educators and the general public. An analogy can be offered with respect to the concept of mainstreaming special education students. Some teachers and administrators argue that placing a mildly mentally handicapped student in a regular mathematics class may be beneficial to the special education student but deleterious to other students. The issue here is similar. Should a disruptive child be allowed to remain in a classroom because a school official has decided that it is in the best interests of this child not to be removed from the class? One suggested activity related to this question is to have students do research out of class on legal precedents that may affect the answer. Especially in the area of mainstreaming, the literature offers legal explanations why the child cannot be deprived of being placed in a "normal" environment if there is no evidence that placement in a special environment results in higher learning outcomes.

6. *What weight should be given to the fact that many parents are also unhappy with the principal's positions on discipline?* This

4

question was included to generate discussion relative to school/community relationships. In this case, the school is located in in an impoverished area. This makes it more likely that school/community relationships are at a low level. Having students state their views permits analysis of how individuals differ in their attitudes regarding parental involvement in elementary school administration. In general, parental dissatisfaction will make the teacher protestations more meaningful.

7. *What information is not provided in this case that you consider important to reaching a decision?* Possible responses include the following:
    a. Knowing whether the principal was doing an effective job in other areas, for example, instructional leadership.
    b. Knowing the level of academic performance of the students in this school compared to other elementary schools in the district.
    c. Knowing whether the principal could document successes, either in this school or in other schools, with his methods.
    d. Knowing whether the principal's attitudes on student discipline were known by central office officials at the time he was assigned to Oliver Wendell Holmes Elementary School.
    e. Knowing the overall organizational climate of the school district (e.g., the disposition toward eradicating conflict).
    f. Knowing whether there are parents and teachers who support the principal.
    g. Knowing the specific policies in the school district relative to discipline.

8. *Identify the advantages and disadvantages of Dr. Danton following the recommendation of the disgruntled teachers to remove Mr. Lattimore as principal.* The possible advantages include:
    a. Resolving the conflict.
    b. Letting the teachers know that their input is valued.
    c. Reinforcing the importance of school/community standards in relation to student discipline.
    d. Possibly avoiding future problems with parents and teachers.
The possible disadvantages include:
    a. Leading administrators to believe that letters of no confidence will lead to their removal.

5

b. Establishing a precedent where the teachers in that school believe they can remove any principal who does not conform to their expectations.

c. Possibly sending a message to the teachers that they should only be concerned with the academic needs of children.

d. Generating conflict between the principals and central administration (e.g., the principals may resent a colleague being removed under these circumstances).

e. Generating a situation where the new principal is very quick to use corporal punishment or issue suspensions.

9. *What can be assumed about the teachers who did not sign the letter of no confidence?* The information in the case provides no indication of why some teachers did not sign the letter. Some may have refused out of conviction (i.e., such letters are not appropriate); some may have refused out of fear; and still others may simply agree with the principal's position.

10. *Can you suggest any positive action that might bring the parents, teachers, and principal together to address this problem?* One concept growing in popularity, especially in urban areas, is the school/community council. Chicago, Illinois, and Hammond, Indiana, are two examples of school systems that have adopted this approach (see Case 8 in the book). The councils are given tremendous latitude in making decisions about how the school will operate. Less formal concepts also may be suggested (for instance, having a series of coffee hours where teachers and parents can exchange views with the principal). Many leaders find that bringing the parties together to discuss the issues works well in conflict situations. In this case, the principal never encouraged his faculty to discuss openly his initiative. It is likely that his behavior with parents has been similar. The principal would benefit from an exchange of views. The teachers and the parents deserve to know what motivates him to initiate change and the principal should know why so many in the school's community oppose his ideas.

11. *Does failing children increase the likelihood that they will be unsuccessful in school?* According to most experts dealing with the topic of at-risk children, failing children is one act that increases the likelihood that the child will never graduate from high school. The reading by Slavin and Madden (1989) on the list in the text will

provide information regarding this matter. The issue of grade retention is one where the principal can produce data to support his position. Yet as previously mentioned, we do not know from the case whether the principal arrived at his position on grade retention because of knowing the research or whether it was merely an instinctive decision.

ADDITIONAL COMMENTS ON CASE 1

Due to the nature of this case, the suggested readings are especially important. Care was taken to balance viewpoints in the reading list. Some readings attack stern discipline and corporal punishment whereas others suggest that get-tough policies can turn around urban schools. For example, the Maynard (1983) article contends that getting tough can actually create problems and the Lowe and Gervais (1984) article presents a case study of an elementary principal who attacks the problems of an unruly student body and apathetic staff by setting, publicizing, and consistently enforcing rules. It is advisable to have students read articles representing both viewpoints. Additionally, it is recommended that all students read the Moore and Cooper (1984) article because it provides insight into how certain variables (e.g., teaching experience) affect approaches to discipline.

This case also addresses another contemporary topic, at-risk students. You may decide to make programming for at-risk youth a focal point when you use this case with your class.

OTHER SUGGESTED ACTIVITIES

1. Invite a psychologist who specializes in behavioral problems and discipline to your class to discuss research on corporal punishment and other forms of discipline.

2. Determine what the laws are in your state regarding corporal punishment.

3. Discuss the principal's assumption that telling teachers he was going to institute change was sufficient.

4. Hold a discussion regarding effective programming for at-risk youth. Among the topics, you may want to illuminate information about what schools do in your state and whether there is any evidence that these practices are effective.

SUGGESTED READINGS:

Alson, A., et al. (1983). Shaping a plan for school improvement: Alternative approaches. *Journal of Staff Development*, 4(1), 25-42.

Auer, M., & Nisenholz, B. (1987). Humanistic processes and bureaucratic structures--Are they compatible? *NASSP Bulletin*, 71(495), 96-101.

Bennett, A. (1986). *Organizational orientation and behavior: A comparative study of elementary school principals*. Unpublished Ed.D. thesis, University of Washington.*

Blase, J. (1984). Teacher coping and school principal behaviors. *Contemporary Education*, 56(1), 21-25.

Blase, J. (1985). The phenomenology of teacher stress: Implications for organizational theory and research. *Administrator's Notebook*, 31(7), 1-4.

Bridgeland, W., & Duane, E. (1987). Elementary school principals and their political settings. *Urban Review*, 19(4), 191-200.

Brown, W., & Payne, T. (1988). Policies/practices in public school discipline. *Academic Therapy*, 23(3), 297-301.*

Burke, T. (1987). *Teacher participation in decision-making*. Unpublished Psy. D. thesis, Rutgers, State University of New Jersey.

Carey, M. (1986). School discipline: Better to be loved or feared? *Momentum*, 17(2), 20-21.

Crooker, R., & Brooker, G. (1986). Classroom control and student outcomes in grades 2 and 5. *American Educational Research Journal*, 23(1), 1-11.

Curwin, R., & Mendler, A. (1988). Packaged discipline programs: Let the buyer beware. *Educational Leadership*, 46(6), 68-71.

Docking, R. (1985). Changing teacher-pupil control ideology and teacher anxiety. *Journal of Education for Teaching*, 11(1), 63-76.

Drake, T., & Roe, W. (1986). *The principalship* (3rd ed.), chap. 16. New York: Macmillan.

Erickson, H. (1988). The boy who couldn't be disciplined. *Principal*, 67(5), 36-37.

Fine, M., & Holt, P. (1983). Corporal punishment in the family: A systems perspective. *Psychology in the Schools*, 20(1), 85-92.

Gottredson, D. (1987). An evaluation of an organizational development approach to reducing school disorders. *Evaluation Review*, 11(6), 739-763.

Guthrie, J., & Reed, R . (1986). *Educational administration and policy*, pp. 325-344. Englewood Cliffs, NJ: Prentice-Hall.

Heitzman, A., & Wiley, D. (1987). School discipline: Problems affecting solutions. *Pointer*, 31(4), 40-44.*

Johnston, G., & Venable, B. (1986). A study of teacher loyalty to the principal: Rule administration and hierarchical influence of principal. *Educational Administration Quarterly*, 22(4) 4-27.

Laughter, K. (1988). Nothing was ever Timothy's fault. *Learning*, 16(9), 38-40.

Lomotey, K., & Swanson, A. (1990). Restructuring school governance: Learning from the experiences of rural and urban schools. In S. Jacobsen & J. Conway (Eds.), *Educational leadership in an age of reform*, pp-82. New York Longman.*

Lowe, R., & Gervais, R. (1984). Tackling a problem school. *Principal*, 63(5), 8-12.

Lunenburg, F. (1987). Another face of school climate. *Illinois Student Journal*, 67(1), 3-10.

Lutz, J., et al. (1987). The Caloosa School: A model for success. *Principal*, 66(4), 18-20.

Madden, N., Slavin, R., Karweit, N., & Livermon, B. (1989). Restructuring the urban elementary school. *Educational Leadership*, 46(5), 14-18.*

Maynard, B. (1983). Is your discipline policy part of your discipline problem? *Executive Educator*, 5(3), 26-27.

McDaniel, T. (1986). School discipline in perspective. *Clearing House*, 59(8), 369-370.

Menacker, J. (1988). Legislating school discipline: The application of a systemwide discipline code for schools in a large urban district. *Urban Education*, 23(1), 12-23.

Menaker, J., Weldon, W., & Hurwitz, E. (1989). School order and safety as community issues. *Phi Delta Kappan*, 71(1), 39-40, 55-56.

Moelis, C. (1988). Banning corporal punishment: A crucial step toward preventing child abuse. *Children's Legal Rights Journal*, 9(33), 2-5.*

Moles, O. (1989). *Student discipline strategies.* Albany, NY: State University of New York Press.*

Moore, W., & Cooper, H. (1984). Correlations between teacher and student background and teacher perceptions of discipline problems and disciplinary techniques. *Psychology in the Schools*, 21(3), 386-392.

Oberg, T. (1986). The ecstasy and the agony: Administrative success on one level does not guarantee success on another. *Journal of Public Relations*, 9(2), 28-31.*

Ornstein, A. (1982). Student disruptions and student rights: An overview. *Urban Education*, 14(2), 83-91.

Reitman, A. (1988). Corporal punishment in schools--The ultimate violence. *Children's Legal Rights Journal*, 9(33), 6-13.

Slavin, R., & Madden, N. (1989). What works for students at-risk: A research synthesis. *Educational Leadership*, 46(5), 4-13.

Snyder, K., & Anderson, R. (1986). *Managing productive schools: Toward an ecology,* pp. 111-123. Orlando, FL: Academic Press College Division.

Thomas, W. (1988). To solve "the discipline problem," mix clear rules with consistent consequences. *American School Board Journal*, 175(6), 30-31.

Vasiloff, B. (1983). The teacher's vital role in developing student discipline. *Momentum*, 13(4), 23-26.

Verble, M. (1985). How to encourage self-discipline. *Learning*, 14(1), 40-42.*

Wynne, E. (1986). Character development: Renewing an old commitment. *Principal*, 65(3), 28-31.

Wynne, E. (1988). Character building: Transmitting values in schools. *Curriculum Review*, 26(1), 18-22.

*readings not included in the text

CASE 2

MANAGEMENT IS MANAGEMENT: OR IS IT?

BACKGROUND INFORMATION

School administrators frequently have social contact with managers in the private sector. Case 2 presents a situation where a young and relatively inexperienced personnel director for a large school system seeks advice from such a friend. Tim's neighbor, Bill, not only is a personnel director for a manufacturing company in the same community, he also is an attorney with expertise in labor relations. Conflict is generated when Tim must choose between the advice of his friend and the judgment of his superintendent--an individual Tim also respects.

The case is presented because it offers an example of how values and beliefs prevalent in private industry often conflict with emerging practices in the public sector. The purpose is not to judge which position is correct; rather, the intent is to contrast how perceptions are formed by leaders in various types of organizations. Additionally, the environment (community) becomes a critical factor in this case.

THE CHALLENGE

Students are apt to select one of the following alternatives when they assume Tim's role in this case:

1. A decision is made to be loyal to the superintendent. As such, the committee is formed and an attempt is made to reach agreement.

2. A decision is made to work for a change in the contract language in hopes that some alternative can be found.

3. A decision is made to insist that the superintendent become personally involved (as Bill had suggested).

4. A decision is made to seek further advice before acting (e.g., studying the issue in greater detail, contacting former professors).

5. A decision is made to withdraw from the situation by either resigning or requesting a new assignment.

The motives for selecting the first option may vary. For example, one individual may elect to be loyal to the superintendent out of fear, while another does so out of respect for his judgment. The advantages and disadvantages of each option are discussed under item 8 in the next section.

Management control in school systems remains a heated question. Some (e.g., Lieberman, 1986) contend that collective bargaining and compromise do not work in the public sector. Students are apt to be divided on this issue; and if this is true, each side should be given the opportunity to defend its position.

KEY ISSUES/QUESTIONS

1. Why do you think Dr. Pryor and Bill have such different opinions about the effectiveness of the school district's policy regarding reduction in force? The superintendent takes a pragmatic stance about the school district and its environment. He views compromise as necessary rather than evil. Bill, on the other hand, is accustomed to working in profit-motivated industries. The climate of private, manufacturing organizations is usually more closed than is the case with public, service organizations (i.e., less willing to interact with the environment). Both academic preparation and experiences lead these two individuals to divergent positions about the existing policy for reductions in the teaching staff. The importance here is to stress the point that schools and metal production plants are vastly different organizations. What works in one setting may not work in the other. Point out the dangers of adopting practices from other organizations without detailed analysis of potential effects.

2. To what extent are principles and practices of management in private industry applicable to public, service organizations? There are practices that are equally effective in both the public and private sector (e.g., efficient maintenance of records). Yet, there are tremendous differences in these organizational environments. In

12

making decisions, a leader has a range of options. The decision can be made in an authoritarian manner or in a completely democratic manner. In private industry, more authoritarian models of decision making are common. Although this also has been true in many school systems, research, theory, and practice suggest that public organizations function more effectively when political realities are confronted and stakeholders are given opportunity for input. Likewise, organizational theory suggests that public institutions should seek interactions with the community and groups that formally or informally affect policy decisions.

3. *Identify factors that differentiate the Shoreline School District from the Shoreline Metal Company.* The following are some of the more conspicuous differences:

   a. the school system has a professionally dominated work force (teachers) whereas the metal company is apt to be composed of unskilled and skilled labor as well as professional managers;

   b. the school system is engaged in providing services--the plant is engaged in manufacturing;

   c. the plant is privately owned--the school district is a public entity;

   d. the plant faces competition--the school district is likely to have a more monopolistic stature (although there is no mention of factors that could create competition, e.g., choice legislation, presence of private education);

   e. the plant is driven by a profit motive--the school district is not; and,

   f. the teachers are in a sense partial owners of the school district if they are taxpayers--workers in the metal plant are not likely to be stockholders.

Each difference cited should be discussed relative to potential impact on leadership style and making decisions.

4. *Should Tim be discussing school business with Bill?* Individuals prone to be management types are likely to criticize Tim for discussing business with Bill. Others will contend that the schools are public entities and that such discussions are appropriate. The point could be made that interactions with the environment (and Tim's discussions with Bill could be classified as such) are healthy for school systems. One could be critical, however, of the

13

fact that only limited interactions occurred (i.e., Tim put too much weight on Bill's opinion and he had no idea if this reflected community sentiments).

5. *Is Bill correct when he makes the judgment that the school administrators cannot rely on past successes in working with the union? Why or why not?* Experience is a factor to be considered in making decisions. It is possible, nevertheless, that a number of circumstances changed between the last time the school administrators and the union officials collaborated on making reduction in force decisions and the time frame of this case. For example, is there new union leadership? Did the union members respond negatively after the last reduction decisions? Did something occur to generate mistrust? Students should be steered away from making a "seat of the pants" decision on this question. They should see the value of raising questions about changing conditions--and ultimately the relationship between existing conditions and an appropriate decision. Such awareness should facilitate the development and analysis of contingencies.

6. *Assess Dr. Pryor's behavior in this case. Do you think his behavior is appropriate?* It is likely that students will disagree with each other on this question. One aspect of the superintendent's behavior that could be criticized is his abrupt judgment that he may have overestimated Tim's ability. The impact of such a statement on a young administrator could be devastating. Some students may see Dr. Pryor as a dynamic leader who has been successful in a very difficult situation. A suggested exercise is to have students list the behaviors and traits they like and dislike in a superintendent. This activity enhances the students' abilities to recognize how their own values and beliefs play a key role in the judgments they make of others.

7. *Identify environmental factors that should be weighed in making a decision.* The brief description of the community in the case portrays an industrial city. Industrial communities tend to reflect the influences of organized labor. Under such circumstances, the majority of the taxpayers may be supportive of a school board and administration attempts to work with unions. Likewise, this is a city with a declining population and a sagging economy. These conditions create a myriad of problems. The turmoil and scarcity of

14

resources in the environmental field, for example, make risk taking more palatable. Practices prevalent in closed organizations are geared toward avoiding failure. Thus when Bill offers his advice, he may be ignoring the environmental conditions that the school district must weigh. Meeting with the union in an attempt to work out reductions in force certainly entails risk. The environment, at least in part, is a factor to be weighed in determining if potential benefits are proportionate to the risk involved.

8. *Identify alternatives that are available to Tim given the circumstances, and evaluate the potential effectiveness of each.* The advantages and disadvantages in the following list are merely examples and not intended to be exhaustive listings.

    a. A decision is made to be loyal to the superintendent. As such, the committee is formed and an attempt is made to reach agreement.

(advantages)

    -likely to reduce tension for Tim

    -permits the superintendent to save face and offers an expression of Tim's loyalty to the superintendent

    -does not violate the contract or attempt to change the contract

(disadvantages)

    -if the decision is made out of fear rather than conviction, Tim is likely to maintain his doubts about the process

    -if the decision is made without weighing changes occurring since the last experience with such committees, the process may encounter difficulties

    -if the procedure fails, Tim may be blamed (either for not heeding Bill's advice or for entering into the process with doubts)

    b. A decision is made to work for a change in the contract language in hopes that some alternative can be found.

(advantages)

    -it buys more time

    -even if he fails, Tim can say that he tried to change things

    -it may prove to be successful

(disadvantages)

    -the union is not very likely to give up this language and an attempt to change it may diminish the relationship between the union and school district officials

15

-the superintendent may view this decision as a rejection of his views

-the action may not be well-received in the community

c. A decision is made to insist that the superintendent become personally involved (as Bill had suggested).

(advantages)

-Tim is not out there alone on the limb

-the superintendent has a greater stake in successful results

(disadvantages)

-this may further diminish the superintendent's confidence in Tim

-the superintendent may refuse and dismiss Tim

-the superintendent becomes involved and is successful and the union has no confidence in Tim (in the future, they will want to deal directly with the superintendent)

d. A decision is made to seek further advice before acting (e.g., studying the issue in greater detail, contacting former professors).

(advantages)

-it buys some time

-the input may prove useful and help Tim come to grips with his own values and beliefs regarding this matter

-it may produce an alternative not originally considered

(disadvantages)

-this may further diminish the superintendent's confidence in Tim

-it may be viewed as "buck passing"

-the advice may only serve to make Tim more undecided

e. A decision is made to withdraw from the situation by either resigning or requesting a new assignment.

(advantages)

-Tim is free of the problem

(disadvantages)

-this is a nonmanagement response for conflict

-it is likely to reflect poorly on Tim and will affect his ability to get another job.

9. *Is Bill correct when he states that unions look out for their members and managers are supposed to look out for the organization?* Many persons, including some school administrators, accept this notion. In reality, leaders are often

16

faced with decisions that address both the needs of individuals and the needs of the organization. In school systems, it is not uncommon for administrators to experience situations where the interests of the school system, the teachers, and the students are in conflict. In large measure, compromise is designed to find a middle ground for the conflicting demands. School systems are human intensive and professionally dominated organizations. Continually ignoring employee needs is likely to create problems. Generalizing about teacher unions can be precarious. Some locals are very sensitive to community conditions. Thus, they may be more prone to compromise the needs and wants of their membership with the needs and wants of the employer. Other locals may be quite rigid and resist any compromise that would not fully support the interests of their members.

OTHER SUGGESTED ACTIVITIES

1. Why are private organizations prone to resist interventions from the environment (e.g., local, state, federal regulations)? See if your students can cite examples of such resistance.

2. Discuss the differences between management and administration. Are they really different concepts?

3. To what extent are managers in private industry questioning their own practices in light of growing international competition? Have your students focus on foreign management practices.

4. Discuss the ways this case might be different if it occurred in a wealthy suburb as opposed to an industrial-based city.

SUGGESTED READINGS:

Allen, R., & Nixon, B. (1988). Developing a new approach to leadership. *Management Education and Development*, 19(3), 174-186.

Burke, R. (1983). Don't be a slave to seniority when developing RIF procedures. *American School Board Journal*, 170(7), 20-21.

Castetter, W. (1986). *The personnel function in educational administration* (4th ed.), pp. 180-183. New York: Macmillan.

Collins, P., & Nelson, D. (1983). Reducing the teacher workforce: A management perspective. *Journal of Law and Education, 12*(2), 249-272.

Conway, J. (1984). The myth, mystery and mastery of participative decision making in education. *Educational Administration Quarterly, 20*(3), 11-40.

Dunnerstick, R. (1987). If RIFs are in the cards for your schools, deal with them deftly. *American School Board Journal, 174*(1), 34.

Eberts, R. (1987). Union-negotiated employment rules and teacher quits. *Economics of Education Review, 6*(1), 15-25.

Estler, S. (1988). Decision making. In N. Boyan (Ed.), *Handbook of research on educational administration*, pp. 321-340. White Plains, NY: Longman.*

Feldt, J. (1986). Markov models and reduction in work force. *New Directions for Institutional Research*, March(49), 29-42.*

Hanson, E. (1985). *Educational administration and organizational behavior* (2nd ed.), pp. 157-162. Boston, MA: Allyn & Bacon.

Hartley, M. (1985). Leadership style and conflict resolution: No manager is an island. *Journal of Cooperative Education, 21*(2), 16-23.

Kowalski, T. (1982). Don't be duped by the industrial mystique. *Executive Educator, 4*(11), 46.

Lieberman, M. (1986). *Beyond public education*, chap. 2. New York: Praeger.

Parkay, F. (1984). A conceptual model for quality oriented educational leadership. *Planning and Changing, 15*(1), 3-9.

Phelan, W. (1983). Staffing policies in times of retrenchment: Teacher opinions. *Peabody Journal of Education, 60*(2), 37-48.*

Snyder, K., & Anderson, R. (1987). What principals can learn from corporate management. *Principal, 66*(4), 22-26.

Threadgill, R. (1988). Analyzing the financial impact of teacher attrition and retirement. *Planning and Changing, 19*(3), 8-13.

Tufts, A. (1984). *Reduction in force: An historical-legal study with recommendations for policy and practice in Connecticut public schools*. Unpublished Ph.D. thesis, University of Connecticut.*

Wengert, M. (1985). *Dismissal of tenured faculty due to financial exigency*. Unpublished Ed.D. thesis, Pepperdine University, California.

Williams, M. (1985). The management of conflict. *New Directions for Higher Education*, 13(2), 33-36.

Wood, C. (1982). Financial exigencies and the dismissal of public school teachers: A legal perspective. *Government Union Review*, 3(4), 49-66.

*readings not included in the text

CASE 3

SETTING HIGHER STANDARDS

BACKGROUND INFORMATION

Prevailing conditions in the environment often spark organizational decisions. This case offers one instance where this occurs. Simpson is a peaceful community that has never really made education a major issue. But activities in the larger environment are affecting local schools. National and state initiatives to reform elementary and secondary schools result in many citizens developing negative perceptions of public education. The relationship between the school district and the environment is only one potential topic for discussion and study in this case. The others include the following:

1. a long-term superintendent who was not required to encounter or manage conflict on any regular basis;

2. ethical and behavioral issues surrounding the acts of the board members;

3. the community's responsibility for what occurs when public boards take such actions; and

4. legal issues surrounding the decisions that were made in this case.

THE CHALLENGE

Assess the decision made by the superintendent. Do you agree with it? What would you have done if you were in his place? It is possible that the superintendent behaved in this way because he was not adept at managing conflict. There are two strong indications of this:

1. After his first confrontation with the new board member, the superintendent really does nothing. In essence, he ignores the source of conflict, probably hoping it will go away.

2. After the board votes to reassign him, he dejectedly announces he will follow the board's wishes.

In one instance he ignores the conflict and in the other he surrenders to it without exploring alternatives. This behavior may be motivated by a strong desire to eradicate the conflict, a learned behavior from being a chief executive in an organization not accustomed to turmoil. Both behaviors exhibited by the superintendent are considered nonmanagement approaches to conflict. Students should be able to recognize that past experiences, the organizational climate of the school district, and the conditions in the general environment converged to affect the superintendent's decisions. In offering alternative behaviors, some of the following could be mentioned:

1. The superintendent should not have ignored his first meeting with the new board member. He should have assessed the potential for trouble and initiated preventive actions.

2. The superintendent should have utilized the impending conflict as a catalyst to seek positive improvements.

3. The superintendent should have expressed a willingness to work with the new board member rather than offering reasons why his ideas could not be adopted in a short time span.

4. The superintendent should have taken the offensive and demanded that the board president act against the new member who was trying to force decisions outside the official operations of the board.

Other alternatives are likely to be offered by students. The value of identifying any option rests with evaluating the potential effectiveness.

KEY ISSUES/QUESTIONS

1. *To what extent were environmental factors (i.e., factors external to the school district as an organization) responsible for what occurred in this case?* Environmental factors play a most important role in this case. The following are the most obvious:
  a. National and state initiatives affect citizen perceptions and heighten interest in school reform.
  b. A community and school district seem unprepared to encounter conflict.
  c. Education is not considered a major issue (e.g., there is virtually is no interest in the board election).
Collectively, these conditions contribute to the challenges faced by the school district and superintendent.

2. *Are public organizations more or less susceptible to environmental influences than private organizations?* Students should be directed to literature explaining why public institutions are more susceptible to environmental influences. Additionally, some discussion should be devoted to the superintendent's responsibility to scan the environment--to remain aware of issues and needs that could affect the school system. Public organizations are owned by taxpayers. This condition alone makes the organization open to environmental influences.

3. *Assess the superintendent's behavior following his first encounter with George Jenkins shortly after the board election. What would you have done differently?* The superintendent's response to his first encounter with George Jenkins is essentially to tell him his ideas cannot be adopted before school starts in the fall. The case offers no indication that the superintendent did anything else. Perhaps he hoped the problem would fade; maybe he thought other board members would reject the initiatives; or, it is possible that he thought the initiatives suggested by Jenkins would simply not be accepted by the public. Students may suggest a range of alternative actions, each of which should be analyzed with regard to effectiveness.

4. *There are at least two major legal issues included in this case*
  a. a school board's ability to reassign a superintendent even

22

though he has two years remaining on his contract, and
    b. a school board's ability to take such action even though the
item is not on the agenda.

Are laws regarding these two matters the same in most states? What are the laws in your home state? Laws regarding matters of board actions and superintendent contracts vary from state to state. Not only should students identify the laws in their own state, but contrasting one state with another is an insightful experience for the students. The question of reassignment also entails compensation. In most states, the superintendent could be reassigned but would be entitled to his administrative salary for the final two years of the contract.

5. *What positive outcomes might result from this incident?* The literature on organizational theory illuminates the potentialities of conflict to produce change, including positive change. Consider some possibilities with regard to this case:

    a. the community takes a much greater interest in the schools and school board elections;

    b. the initiatives suggested by the board member spawn the creation of study committees that seek improvements for the school district;

    c. the school administrators recognize the need to become more adept at managing conflict; and

    d. the professional staff decides to take a proactive rather than reactive stance toward formulating recommendations.

There are a multitude of other possibilities. The critical point for students rests with understanding that conflict can be used to produce change and that change can be either good or bad.

6. *To what extent is the community at large responsible for what occurred in this case?* A community must assume responsibility for its own governance. This is true of schools as well as other service agencies. The fact that there was little interest in the board election allowed two persons to be seated on the board without stating their values and beliefs to the public. In instances where school boards behave in irrational or unethical ways, it is the community that most often can correct the situation. In a democratic society, a community should accept responsibility for its local school board.

7. *Identify all of the superintendent's available options regarding his reassignment.* Among the possibilities available to the superintendent regarding his job status are the following:
    a. He could retain legal counsel and fight the decision.
    b. He could resign.
    c. He could seek to negotiate a cash settlement and leave the district.
    d. He could ask the board to reconsider based on a willingness to work with them to seek their goals.
    e. He could ask key individuals or agencies to investigate the matter (e.g., the state superintendents' association, the state school board's association, the state department of education).
Have students evaluate the potential effectiveness of each option.

8. *Assess Dr. Swaim's behavior. Should he have done something after receiving his first visit from George Jenkins? Should he have resigned from the board?* For the most part, Dr. Swaim acted much like the superintendent. He basically ignored his first encounter with George Jenkins. If nothing else, the board president should have discussed the appropriateness of board members acting alone and outside of official board meetings. Students are likely to disagree as to whether Dr. Swaim was right in resigning. Some will contend it was the coward's way out. Others will perceive it as a noble act. Discussing the reasons why students take one position or another is encouraged.

9. *Identify potential motivators with regard to George Jenkins's behavior. Why did he run for the board? What exactly is he trying to accomplish?* Among the possible reasons why George Jenkins ran for the school board are the following:
    a. He is frustrated by his experience on the governor's task force to do at the local level what he was unable to do at the state level.
    b. He is doing this as a personal favor to the governor, who wants to prove that his ideas could work.
    c. He is an individual with a big ego.
    d. He has political ambitions and views the school board as an opportunity to make a name for himself.
    e. He truly believes in the reforms he is advocating; thus, he is driven by conviction.

24

Knowing what motivated him can be extremely important for the superintendent. The alternatives that might be pursued to eradicate such a situation could be affected by this information. The linkage between individual motivation and alternative solutions should be made clear to the students. Additionally, knowing what motivated him is necessary information regarding a clear perspective of what he intends to accomplish.

10. What are some possible explanations why three of the five returning board members voted with Jenkins and Potter? Three of the five board members not involved in the recent school board election supported the motion to make George Jenkins board president and to reassign the superintendent. Possible reasons for this behavior include the following:

    a. The three were politically intimidated by Jenkins.

    b. The three admired Jenkins, especially his willingness to take risks.

    c. The three really were not supportive of the superintendent or current conditions but were afraid to express their feelings prior to Jenkins being elected to the board.

    d. The three did not like controversy and viewed supporting Jenkins as the "easy way out."

Students should discuss the importance of identifying the reason(s) why these three acted the way they did. Additionally, discussion can focus on reasons why one dominating figure can change the direction of an entire school board.

OTHER SUGGESTED ACTIVITIES

1. Have students evaluate the appropriateness of the reform recommendations offered by the new board member.

2. Have students develop recommended policy statements that would have prevented a new member from acting alone even prior to being officially seated on the board.

3. Debate the soundness of a policy that permits a board member not to be seated for a full year after being elected. Why would such a policy ever be tolerated?

SUGGESTED READINGS:

Bacal, E. (1986). Learn not to burn, or fulminate over school board trouble. *American School Board Journal,* 173(5), 29-30.

Bacharach, S., et al. (1986). The work environment and school reform. *Teachers College Record,* 88, 241-256.

Carr, R. (1988). Second-wave reforms crest at local initiative. *School Administrator,* 45(7), 16-18.

Cooper, H. (1989). Synthesis of research on homework. *Educational Leadership,* 47(3), 85-91.*

Edwards, M. (1988). Setting school board goals: A model for accountability. *Educational Horizons,* 66(3), 117-118.

Ginsberg, R., & Berry, B. (1990). Experiencing school reform: The view from South Carolina. *Phi Delta Kappan,* 71, 549-552.*

Henson, K. (1986). Reforming America's public schools. *USA Today,* 114(3), 75-77.

Hopkins, R. (1989). How to survive and succeed as the chief school executive. *The School Administrator,* 9(46), 15-17.

Hoy, W., & Ferguson, J. (1985). A theoretical framework and exploration of organizational effectiveness of schools. *Educational Administration Quarterly,* 21(2), 117-134.

Krajewski, R. (1983). Nine ways a superintendent can corral a maverick board member. *American School Board Journal,* 170(11), 29-30.

Lawler, E. (1985). Education, management style, and organizational effectiveness. *Personnel Psychology,* 38(1), 1-26.*

Lintz, M. (1987). *Practices and techniques to improve school-community relations and develop confidence in the public schools.* Unpublished Ed.D. thesis, University of Tennessee.*

MacDougall, C. (1988). Boards need education, too! *Updating School Board Policies,* 19(5), 1-2.

Martinez, A. (1987). *Conflict between school boards and superintendents and strategies employed for resolution.* Unpublished Ed.D. thesis, University of Nevada, Las Vegas.*

McKenna, M. (1986). *Community attitudes and opinions in relation to school reform: A teaching unit.* Unpublished Ed.D. thesis, Teachers College, Columbia University.*

Namit, C. (1987). How a crisis meeting can control school board trouble. *American School Board Journal,* 174(9), 36-37.

Niblett, S. (1985). *Superintendent turnover and organizational change*. Unpublished Ph.D. thesis, University of California, Santa Barbara.

Peterson, P. (1985). Did the education commissions say anything? *Education and Urban Society*, 17(2), 126-144.

Rada, R. (1984). Community dissatisfaction and school governance. *Planning and Changing*, 15(4), 234-247.

Roeder, G. (1987). *A study of the reasons why Michigan school superintendents were dismissed or encouraged to leave their positions between 1980 and 1985*. Unpublished Ph.D. thesis, University of Michigan, Ann Arbor.

Seashore, K., et al. (1988). Knowledge use and school improvement. *Curriculum Inquiry*, 18(1), 33-62.

Shanker, A. (1985). The reform reports: Reaction from the front lines. *Education and Urban Society*, 17(2), 215-222.

Slaughter, S. (1988). Academic freedom and the state: Reflections on the uses of knowledge. *Journal of Higher Education*, 59(3), 241-262.

Turlington, R. (1985). How testing is changing education in Florida. *Educational Measurement Issues and Practices*, 4(2), 9-11.

Wimpelberg, R., & Ginsberg, R. (1985). Are school districts responding to A Nation at Risk? *Education and Urban Society*, 17(2), 196-203.

Yeakey, C., & Johnston, G. (1985). High school reform: A critique and a broader construct of social reality. *Education and Urban Society*, 17(2), 157-170.

*readings not included in the text

CASE 4

TOO MANY SCHOOLS

BACKGROUND INFORMATION

Case 4 is a complex situation that remains unresolved for the school district. School consolidation in the late 1950s and early 1960s eliminated many small school systems in this country; however, the governance compromises typically assured small communities representation on the reorganized school boards. This case illustrates the potency of political dynamics affecting major educational decisions. In the face of overwhelming evidence that one or two high schools should be closed, the school board refuses to act for fear of angering residents. The case is made more interesting by the fact that the board steadfastly supports the superintendent in all other matters and has gone to great lengths to keep him in the school system. Furthermore, the superintendent's efforts to close schools are supported by the teachers' union.

THE CHALLENGE

Students basically have four options in responding to the challenge in this case:

1. Leave the school system, recognizing that progress is impossible.

2. Heed the board's advice and leave the matter alone until enrollment patterns change or the situation becomes an absolute crisis.

3. Continue efforts to change the minds of the board members.

4. Ask the state department of education to intervene in the matter.

Students who opt to stay and work to change the positions of board members should be asked to outline the strategy they would employ.

28

Students opting for the other choices should be asked to outline the perceived advantages and disadvantages of their behavior.

KEY ISSUES/QUESTIONS

1. *Identify Dr. Bellman's options. What do you perceive to be the advantages and disadvantages of each?* As mentioned in the previous section, there are four basic responses to this case. The following outlines some advantages and disadvantages for each:
    a. Leaving the district
(advantages)
        -The superintendent can go to another environment where he can be more productive.
        -The next superintendent may be able to have more leverage change.
        -The departure of the superintendent may shock the board into acting.
(disadvantages)
        -Some would argue that the superintendent is running away from the problem.
        -There is no assurance that another superintendent will command the respect given to the current superintendent.
        -It is likely that any solution will be deferred further and educational programs will suffer if there is a change in the superintendency.
    b. Heeding the board's advice
(advantages)
        -It gets the superintendent off the "hot seat."
        -It is apt to strengthen the superintendent's relationship with the board and the community.
(disadvantages)
        -Many would consider this to be a "non-management" solution. That is, the superintendent is letting the board lead him rather than vice versa.
        -Neglecting the problem could result in many negative repercussions that may ultimately be blamed on the superintendent (e.g., court intervention in racial distribution, state control of the district because of poor financial management).

29

-The superintendent may loose the respect of his professional staff.

-The students suffer in the end because identified problems are not eradicated.

c. Working to change the board members

(advantages)

-The superintendent capitalizes on his stature with the board to work toward enlightening hem. He may be the best hope for bringing about change.

-This choice will require a constant updating of data that should prove beneficial when any solution is finally selected.

-The superintendent may enhance his image with his professional staff. He will be perceived as a "fighter."

(disadvantages)

-The experience could prove to be frustrating.

-If board members remain stubborn, they may eventually become angry with the superintendent for continuing to prod them on this issue.

-The board members may leave and efforts to change their positions will end in failure (i.e., the current board members will leave the board only to be replaced by others who hold the same views).

d. Bringing in the state department

(advantages)

-This could place political pressure on the school board members.

-It would enlighten the public that the state has a vested responsibility in assuring the vitality of local public education.

(disadvantages)

-The board could become angry at the superintendent.

-Attempts by state officials to mandate change may make local residents even more adamant to fight school closings.

There are many other advantages and disadvantages that students may articulate in discussing the superintendent's options. Those listed here provide a sampling of reactions.

2. *Why do you believe the school board members are reluctant to close a high school?* The reasons are likely to vary from one school

board member to another. Some may have political ambitions. They do not want to alienate the voters in any way. Some may be individuals who simply cannot handle conflict. They would rather have the superintendent angry at them than to have their neighbors attacking them. Others may believe that the small schools should stay open regardless of the cost. Finally, some may have decided to pass the problem to the next generation of board members. Myron Lieberman, for example, argues that public boards often make poor decisions because they know they will not be held accountable for the consequences (see his book, <u>Beyond Public Education</u>, Praeger, 1986).

3. *Was it a good idea to have university professors complete the planning studies that led to the recommendations for school closings?* Individual school administrators vary markedly in their views toward the use of consultants. Some view the use of consultants as an indicator that they are incapable of performing their own duties. This question should lead to a detailed discussion regarding the advantages and disadvantages of using consultants. The advantages of objectivity, knowledge, and experience and the disadvantages of cost and possible negative public reactions should be stressed.

4. *The parents who object to closing a high school retained two consultants to testify that small high schools are better than large high schools. Do you agree with this assessment? What evidence can you provide to support your answer?* Arguments surrounding school size have not subsided. There is little doubt that smaller schools offer students greater opportunities for leadership and participation (e.g., in athletics, clubs). Some psychologists contend that small schools provide students a greater sense of belonging. On the other hand, small schools often cannot provide a comprehensive curriculum and they are expensive to operate. Most experts suggest that a high school with an enrollment of between 800 and 1,500 pupils is ideal. At 800, the school is of sufficient size to offer a rather broad curriculum and at 1,500 it is not so large as to alienate some students. In truth, there is no right or wrong answer to this issue. Individual values and beliefs again play a critical role in one's position on this matter. It is vital, however, that students realize that small schools are defensible if one only looks at issues such as social and psychological adjustments for pupils. They become less

defensible when administrative considerations such as curriculum scope, cost, and facility utilization are infused into the analysis.

5. *Why do you believe that the teachers' union is supporting Dr. Bellman in this matter?* In this case, the teachers support the superintendent for two primary reasons: (1) he is committed to raising their salaries and he is able to link this goal to the facility issue, and (2) he is able to point out how curricular inequities are starting to affect working conditions for individual teachers (e.g., teachers at the smaller high schools had many more preparations than the teachers at the larger high schools).

6. *Why do taxpayers often fight to retain schools in small rural communities?* Small farming communities are disappearing across the country. Schools are often perceived as critical to keeping small towns alive. Many residents believe that if the school closes, remaining businesses will eventually move out. Additionally, there often is an emotional attachment to schools in these settings (i.e., parents want their children to go to the same school they attended). Finally, parents often fight to minimize the distance between home and school. In this particular case, there is some speculation that increases in minority enrollments also play a part in taxpayer opposition to school closings. Some schools in the district have large minority enrollments and others have virtually none.

7. *The state in which this occurred utilizes a program of total local funding for capital outlay. What are the range of options for financing facility projects that exist among the fifty states? Did the program of total local funding affect decisions in this case?* States vary in the way they mandate or permit capital outlay to be financed. Many states still have laws requiring virtually all of the revenue to be generated at the local level. Some states have moved to shared financing between local and state revenues. Finally, a very small number of states have programs of total state financing. In this case, one could conclude that total local funding permitted the school district to continue spending money on capital development even though there were some indicators that student growth would not continue. It is possible that state participation in funding could have resulted in more requirements for long-range planning and a higher level of caution.

32

8. *If you were Dr. Bellman, would you emphasize or deemphasize the fact that the teachers' union supported your position?* In part, the answer to this question is predicated on the overall choice of the superintendent in how to deal with this matter. Also, the case does not reveal how the board and community perceive the teachers' union. Students should be asked to justify their response to this question by detailing information that led to a specific conclusion. Additionally, they should be asked to list the advantages and disadvantages of their action.

9. *What is the relevance of the minority enrollment patterns present in the school district?* The concentration of minorities in one location suggests that external interventions are highly likely in the future. For example, the school district may end up with two virtually all-black schools in a district that has less than a 15 percent minority population. Legal action by advocate groups, for example, the National Association for the Advancement of Colored People (NAACP), may be suggested. In addition to legal ramifications, you may want to point out to students that there are curricular issues as well. For example, should the school district intensify its effort to offer multicultural education? Lastly, there are social and political issues to consider. What kind of message does the school district give to children if it does not take a positive approach to racial integration?

10. *What is the relevance of curricular inequities among the five high schools in this case?* Because of enrollment differences, some high schools offer three and four foreign languages whereas others offer only one. Similar inequities are emerging in basic science and mathematics classes. For example, only one out of five high schools offers advanced chemistry. This situation could lead to legal problems if some parents decide that children do not have access to equal educational opportunities. In larger school systems, equity in educational experiences is a pervasive concern.

11. *Should a community have the right to say no to school closings or should the state step in and play a role in this matter?* This question is designed to generate a discussion of state responsibility for public education. How far should a local community be allowed to go in making decisions about school closings, boundaries, curriculum, and the like? In many states, the local school district

must obtain approval for school facility projects from the state department of education. This approval is used as leverage to assure that proper planning has occurred. But such controls do not exist for school closings. You may want to have students debate whether the state officials should be allowed to mandate closing schools due to declining enrollment.

OTHER SUGGESTED ACTIVITIES

1. Invite a superintendent who has recently had to close a school to visit your class.

2. Invite school board members to your class and engage them in a discussion of factors they identify as important in considering school closings.

3. Identify schools that have been closed in your state and try to determine the major factors leading to those decisions.

SUGGESTED READINGS:

Boyd, W., & Wheaton, D. (1983). Conflict management in declining school districts. *Peabody Journal of Education*, 50(2), 25-36.

Bozza, R. (1985). *Declining enrollments and school closings: The management of political conflict*. Unpublished Ed.D. thesis, Rutgers, State University of New Jersey.

Brown, R., et al. (1985). An exploratory study of contextual factors as influences on school board evaluation information needs for decision making. *Educational Evaluation and Policy Analysis*, 7(4), 437-445.*

Chabotar, K. (1987). Use of financial forecasting in educational retrenchment. *Journal of Education Finance*, 12, 351-368.

Chabotar, K., & Dentler, R. (1985). Cutback management planning assistance for local public school systems. *Planning and Changing*, 16, 223-240.

Cibulka, J. (1987). Theories of education budgeting: Lessons from management of decline. *Educational Administration Quarterly*, 23(4), 7-40.

Crespo, M., & Hache, J. (1982). The management of decline in education: The case of Quebec. *Educational Administration Quarterly*, 18(1), 75-99.

Darling, J., & Ishler, R. (1989-90). Strategic conflict management problem-oriented approach. *National Forum of Educational Administration and Supervision Journal*, 7(1), 87-103.

Dwyer, J. (1985). *School closing decisions: Cases and concepts.* Unpublished Ed.D. thesis, Indiana University, Bloomington.*

Guthrie, J., & Reed, R. (1986). *Educational administration and policy,* pp. 52-55. Englewood Cliffs, NJ: Prentice-Hall.

Hayden, J. (1986). Crisis at the helm. *The School Administrator*, 43(10), 17-19.

Kowalski, T. (1989). *Planning and managing schools facilities,* pp. 30-32. New York: Praeger.*

Lieberman, M. (1986). *Beyond public education.* New York: Praeger.*

Love, D. (1987). *Criteria and processes used in school-closing decisions by school corporations in Indiana.* Unpublished Ed.D. thesis, Indiana University, Bloomington.

Mertz, C. (1986). Conflict and frustration for school board members. *Urban Education*, 20(4), 397-418.

Newman, D., et al. (1987). Factors influencing the decision-making process: An examination of the effect of contextual variables. *Studies in Educational Evaluation*, 13(2), 199-209.

Nocera, E. (1986). *A study of school closing in two school systems in relation to decision-making and organizational and political impacts.* Unpublished Ph.D. thesis, University of Connecticut.

Owens, R., & Lewis, E. (1976). Managing participation in organizational decisions. *Group and Organizational Studies*, 1, 55-56.

Pankake, A., & Bailey, M. (1986). Managing decline in public schools. *Urban Education*, 21, 180-188.

Vroom, V., & Jago, A. (1988). *The new leadership: Managing participation in organizations,* pp. 54-65. Englewood Cliffs, NJ: Prentice-Hall.

Yukl, G. (1989). *Leadership in organizations* (2nd ed.), pp. 58-60. Englewood Cliffs, NJ: Prentice-Hall.

*readings not included in the text

CASE 5

AN ASSISTANT PRINCIPAL WHO DOES NOT FIT THE IMAGE

BACKGROUND INFORMATION

Can community and/or organizational expectations be so strong that they dictate dress codes for teachers and administrators? To what extent does the organizational climate of a school district assume the values and beliefs of its community environment? These questions are central to this case. A highly successful principal is asked to remain silent as his assistant is reassigned to a teaching position. He is asked to remain silent even though he has consistently rated his assistant very high and recommended him for maximum merit increases. The principal views the assistant as a vital member of the administrative team. The assistant is willing to assume the managerial tasks related to administering the high school permitting the principal to engage in other leadership activities. In the eyes of the superintendent and associate superintendent, however, the assistant principal does not meet the desired image of a school administrator in their district.

Case 5 raises a number of questions regarding the performance evaluation of a high school assistant principal. There are two other areas that can be developed as primary areas of study: (1) leadership expectancy theories; and (2) the effects of organizational climate on conformity in personal traits of leaders.

THE CHALLENGE

There are strong indications that this is a school district embracing many values of a highly bureaucratic private corporation. For example, the superintendent has only limited contact with principals even though this is a relatively small school district. The exercise of legitimate power by the superintendent is also evident. Thus, a student should be expected to weigh the implications of organizational climate before responding to the challenge. If the principal decides to conform with the request made by his superintendent, he may fortify his position administratively (i.e., he may be viewed positively by the superintendent) but face other consequences. Beyond ethical and personal considerations, the principal may be faced with uncomfortable circumstances if the reassigned assistant principal decides to take legal action against the school officials. How will he justify not protecting his assistant given the evaluative data that exist?

If the principal rejects the wishes of his superiors, he faces other difficulties. It is reasonable to assume that fighting to protect his assistant principal will generate enormous conflict. If the superintendent has the confidence of the school board, opposition by the principal could result in a deterioration of the relationship between the principal and superintendent.

At first glance, some students may surmise that there are only three choices in this matter. Surrender to the superintendent, fight him on this issue, or withdraw from the conflict (e.g., resign the principalship). There are several other alternatives. For example, a skillful principal may elect to delay the decision in hopes of continuing a dialogue with his superiors regarding the effective performance of his assistant. Perhaps if they were better informed of what this individual does, they would be more reasonable in their judgments. Another option might be for the principal to suggest that he will work with his assistant to improve his personal appearance. The principal could argue that it is better for the organization to improve the appearance of a highly effective administrator than to employ someone who has the proper appearance but may lack skills and experience.

KEY ISSUES/QUESTIONS

1. *To what extent do you believe the nature of the community plays a role in this case?* School districts are influenced by their environments. This is a community in which many corporate executives reside. Thus prevailing values and beliefs in corporate life are likely to have some effect on leadership behaviors in the public schools. If this incident occurred in a rural setting, the issue of dress standards for an assistant principal may not have become a major issue.

You may want to use this case to talk about trait theory as well. Why do some individuals equate effective management with personal appearance? What has been the history of trait theory in educational administration? Is there any value in trait theory?

2. *What aspects of organizational theory are helpful in determining why the personal appearance of an assistant principal is a critical element in this case?* Many highly bureaucratic organizations demand conformity. In private business, concepts such as "dress for success" and "standard blue suits" have emerged as expectancies for executives. Bureaucracies are highly dependent on rules, so conformity in external behavior is deemed important. Encourage a discussion on the question of the current status of bureaucratic values in public school systems.

3. *What does Allen have to gain by agreeing to do what the superintendent and associate superintendent are requesting?* He can strengthen his political stature in the organization. He will be viewed as a "team player." He already enjoys a high level of support from his superiors and he may be able to strengthen that support by accommodating them in this matter. In some ways, the principal is similar to the superintendent (e.g., he delegates many functions to his assistant). If the principal is an upwardly mobile person, he may conform simply to assure a positive recommendation from his superiors. Yet, these gains may come at a heavy cost. A myriad of ethical and professional questions can emerge if the principal simply goes along with his superiors.

4. *What options does Allen have, if any, beyond either agreeing or not agreeing to what his superiors have asked of him?* There are several: (1) resigning from the school system; (2) working to change his superiors' perceptions; (3) working to change his assistant's personal appearance; (4) working to change the evaluation system to assure that there is agreement on performance objectives before the evaluations occur; and   (5) a combination of all of the above except (1). The principal could take the position that the evaluation of the assistant principal should be based on performance. If the superintendent and associate superintendent want to stipulate expectations, those expectations should be infused into next year's evaluative cycle. In this fashion, the assistant principal is given ample time to correct problems.

5. *Evaluate the administrative structure (line and staff) in this district. What do you like about it? What do you dislike?* A variety of responses can be expected. One topic that deserves focused attention entails the relative isolation of the superintendent from building level administrators. Principals do not report to him; in fact, they rarely see him. If students exhibit disagreements relative to their approval of the organizational structure of the school district, it is advisable to engage them in a discussion of why these differences exist. For example, why would some students want to be a principal in a school district where they have frequent contact with the superintendent and other students prefer to work in a very formal, structured environment where contact with central office personnel is limited?

6. *To what extent is the line-and-staff relationship among the administrative staff a contributing factor to this case?* There is no way to absolutely conclude that the line-and-staff relationship is a contributing factor; however, there is circumstantial evidence indicating that the superintendent's isolation from the principal probably contributed to a lack of communications regarding the job performance of the assistant principal. If the superintendent is going to play an important role in the evaluation of assistant principals and principals, then he should be involved in the initial goal-setting sessions for these individuals. In this case, it is evident that the superintendent neither directly nor indirectly (i.e., through the associate superintendent) informed the principal of his concerns in sufficient time so that remediation could have been attempted.

7. *How do you assess the role of the associate superintendent in this case?* There is no way of knowing if the concerns relative to the assistant principal were discussed by the superintendent and associate superintendent over a period of time. If they were, the associate superintendent was certainly lax in not attempting to work toward a plan of remediation. In any event, some students may criticize the associate superintendent for going along with the reassignment to classroom teaching. Many students will see this situation as being grossly unfair to the assistant principal because: (1) he probably does not even know that this concern exists, and (2) he is not to be given any opportunity to exhibit improvement. In addition, the associate superintendent can be criticized because she approved maximum merit increases in the past for the assistant principal without

ever raising any concerns relative to his performance. Now, she is willing to side with the superintendent in removing him from his administrative post.

8. *To what extent did Allen err by assuming that this would be a routine conference?* Although many students are apt to criticize Allen for accepting the conference as a routine step in the evaluation process, there is no evidence in this case that suggests he should have expected something else. A discussion could be generated regarding the steps the principal could have taken to avoid surprises in the evaluative conference. For example, he could have asked the associate superintendent at various intervals during the school year if there were any concerns relating to job performance. If this had been done, the principal could have complained that the appearance of the assistant principal had never been brought to his attention in such discussions. The value of periodic conferences in evaluation cycles can be highlighted here.

9. *Some administrators might defend the action of the superintendent and assistant superintendent on the grounds that it is best to "act swiftly and forcefully" in controversial situations. Do you agree?* This question provides an opportunity to discuss the value of theory and reflection in decision making. What are the advantages of weighing alternative courses of action? Does the administrator fully understand the possible advantages and disadvantages of a decision before it is made? Often there is some advantage to acting swiftly, but this advantage ought to be weighed against possible disadvantages and the advantages of other options.

10. *Discuss the differences between summative and formative evaluation. To what extent are the superintendent and associate superintendent supporting both processes?* The information provided in the case leads one to conclude that the top two administrators in this district care very little about formative evaluation. Two primary pieces of evidence support this contention: (1) there is no concern voiced about helping the assistant principal become a better administrator, and (2) the primary concern expressed by the superintendent does not relate to job performance, but to personal appearance. There is no indication that the central office administrators accept responsibility for improving employee performance. Additionally, no attempt is made to link the positive

performance assessment of the principal with the assessment of his assistant.

OTHER SUGGESTED ACTIVITIES

1. Have the students determine if the school districts in which they are (or were) employed have any standards of dress for building level administrators. Are these standards included in the formal evaluation process?

2. Discuss the value of reaching consensus on goals at the beginning of the evaluation cycle.

3. Have the students identify existing laws in your state relative to reassigning an administrator to classroom teaching.

4. Identify possible reasons why the superintendent in this district does not have the principals reporting directly to him.

A FINAL THOUGHT

The intended action of the superintendent raises some rather interesting questions regarding differing expectations of administrators and teachers. If the assistant principal's personal appearance is deemed unsatisfactory for an administrator, why is it acceptable for a teacher? There seems to be a double standard. In fact, this condition exists in many school districts. A male teacher may not wear a tie and coat and nothing is said; but if an administrator dresses casually, it causes great alarm. This is an interesting topic for discussion.

SUGGESTED READINGS:

Aidala, G. (1986). *A study of career bound and place bound assistant principals in the public secondary schools of New York state and a comparison of their levels of job satisfaction.* Unpublished Ed.D. thesis, State University of New York, Albany.

Drake, T., & Roe, W. (1986). *The principalship* (3rd ed.), pp. 19-29. New York: Macmillan.

Fulton, O. (1987). Basic competencies of the assistant principal. *NASSP Bulletin*, 71(501), 52.

Hamner, T., & Turk, J. (1987). Organizational determinants of leader behavior and authority. *Journal of Applied Psychology*, 72, 647-682.

Hanson, E. (1985). *Educational administration and organizational behavior* (2nd ed.), pp. 168-169. Boston: Allyn & Bacon.

Harrison, W., & Peterson, K. (1988). Evaluation of principals: The process can be improved. *NASSP Bulletin*, 72(508), 1-4.

Hemphill, J., Griffiths, D., & Frederiksen, N. (1962). *Administrative performance and personality*. New York: Teachers College Press, Columbia University.*

Hoy, W., & Forsyth, P. (1986). *Effective supervision: Theory into practice*, pp. 168-169. New York: Random House.

Hoy, W., & Miskel, C. (1987). *Educational administration: Theory, research and practice* (3rd ed.), pp. 76-79. New York: Random House.

Hoy, W., Newland, W., & Blaxovsky, R. (1977). Subordinate loyalty to superior, esprit, and aspects of bureaucratic structure. *Educational Administration Quarterly*, 13(1), 71-85.

Immegart, G. (1988). Leadership and leader behavior. In N. Boyan (Ed.), *Handbook of research on educational administration*, pp. 259-278. White Plains, NY: Longman.

Lang, R. (1986). The hidden dress code dilemma. *Clearing House*, 5(6), 277-279.

Licata, J. (1983). Systemic appraisal of educational leadership personnel. In E. Zapulla (Ed.), *Evaluating administrative performance: Current trends and techniques*, pp. 281-303. Belmont, CA: Star Publishing.*

McCarthy, M. (1987). *The work-life of the assistant principal in public comprehensive high schools*. Unpublished Ed.D. thesis, University of Massachusetts.

McPherson, R., & Crowson, R. (1987). Sources of constraints and opportunities for discretion in the principalship. In J. Lane & H. Walberg (Eds.), *Effective school leadership*, pp. 129-156. Berkeley, CAMcCutchan.

Manatt, R. (1987). Lessons from a comprehensive performance appraisal project. *Educational Leadership*, 44(7), 8-14.

Newell, C. (1978). *Human behavior in educational administration*, Chap. 6. Englewood Cliffs, NJ: Prentice-Hall.

Niehouse, O. (1988). Leadership concepts for the principal: A practical approach. *NASSP Bulletin*, 72(505), 50-52.*

Norton, M., & Kriekard, J. (1987). Real and ideal competencies for the assistant principal. *NASSP Bulletin*, 71(501), 23-30.

Ogden, J. (1986). *The development and analysis of employment dimensions predicated upon the utilization of Egon Brunswik's Lens Model.* Unpublished Ph.D. thesis, University of Northern Colorado.*

Peterson, K. (1984). Mechanisms of administrative control over managers educational organizations. *Administrative Science Quarterly*, 29, 573-597.

Wood, C., Nicholson, E., & Findley, D. (1985). *The secondary school principal: Manager and supervisor* (2nd ed.), Chap. 4. Boston: Allyn & Bacon.

Yukl, G. (1989). *Leadership in organizations* (2nd ed.), pp. 151-157, 174-191. Englewood Cliffs, NJ: Prentice-Hall.

*readings not included in the text

CASE 6

PROGRAM EXPANSION OR BUDGET CUTS?

BACKGROUND INFORMATION

Many superintendents encounter surprises during the first few months in a new position. In fact, well-traveled superintendents, that is, those who have held several different superintendencies, often expect that they were not told everything about the district during the employment interviews. In Case 6, we have an administrator assuming her first superintendency in what is perceived to be "an almost perfect district." Not only is she caught off guard in finding out there is a financial problem, she quickly discovers that the administrative staff is less than unanimous in supporting a solution to the problem.

In part, the case is made more perplexing because members of the administrative staff have gone on record as supporting four different solutions. The superintendent has to reach a decision regarding a recommendation to the board of education and she is concerned about possibly alienating some of her staff members in the process. The infusion of material related to conflict theories, especially those directly related to decision making, will make this case more meaningful for your students.

THE CHALLENGE

Superintendents frequently find themselves caught between demands for programs and limited resources. Input the superintendent is receiving from her staff is mixed. The following are among the available alternatives:

a. Institute the new programs despite financial concerns.

b. Institute one, but not both new programs.

c. Refuse to institute either program due to financial problems.

d. Defer a decision until the matter can be studied more fully.

e. Create a special study committee to examine the issue more fully.

f.Institute the two new programs while simultaneously eradicating other programs so that funds are made available.

KEY ISSUES/QUESTIONS

1. *Are the two elementary principals correct when they warn the superintendent that this is a politically explosive issue? What information in the case leads you to your conclusion on this question?* Students who respond to this query in the affirmative are likely to point to the nature of the community and the process utilized to initiate additions to the curricula. University Hills is a community composed of well-educated citizens and the case points out that parents are highly interested in the schools. Often communities of this type believe that public education should be responsive to community needs and wants. Thus, the petition method is selected to exhibit to the school board that the community truly wants a program.

The school district also has a history of involving teachers in curriculum studies. The continuation of this process over time suggests that teacher views are considered important. Thus program recommendations emanating from this process also are likely to have a political impact on school board members.

Students who respond in the negative may contend that the public and the board have not been properly apprised of financial conditions. Thus, they may believe that the community will be understanding if the superintendent is able to adequately explain why it is not feasible to pursue the two new initiatives.

2. *Identify the advantages and disadvantages of each of the positions advocated by members of the administrative staff.* Students generally produce some creative responses in identifying advantages and disadvantages. Among the more common that could be expected are the following:

Position A: Do not institute the two new programs and cut $50,000 from the travel and equipment budgets.
   (advantages)
      -It will provide the needed financial relief.
      -It appears to address financial concerns with a minimum of effect on existing programs.

-It would make some believe that the superintendent is a good manager who makes pragmatic decisions based on resources.

(disadvantages)

-It could become a real political problem.

-It could make some believe that the superintendent will be controlled by the business manager.

-It could be perceived that the superintendent is prone to make quick decisions about matters in which she has limited information.

Position B: Leave the new programs alone and cut out some athletic programs at the middle and high schools sufficient to cover projected deficits.

(advantages)

-It would resolve the financial problem faced by the district.

-It may be perceived as a bold act by parents and teachers who support the two new initiatives for elementary schools.

(disadvantages)

-It may cause a political reaction far greater than one that might be expected if the two new initiatives are not pursued.

-Some may judge that the superintendent is prone to knee-jerk reactions.

-It may be perceived that the superintendent is influenced by recommendations of female administrators on her staff.

Position C: Form a special study committee and do not institute any new programs or cut any existing programs until study is completed.

(advantages)

-It may be perceived as an unbiased and reasonable alternative.

-It may be the safest alternative politically.

-It gives the superintendent more time to study the issues and facts.

(disadvantages)

-It may be perceived as the easy way out for the superintendent.

-It may send signals to employees and the board that the superintendent is willing to let committees handle difficult decisions.

-Because no cuts are made immediately, this alternative may only compound financial problems.

Position D: The superintendent should make the decision and all administrative staff should be supportive of that decision.

(advantages)

-It enhances the legitimate authority of the superintendent.

-It reduces the likelihood that administrators will be arguing among themselves publicly (i.e., the superintendent may require everyone to fall in line or face the consequences).

-It may enhance the perception that the superintendent is willing to make difficult decisions.

(disadvantages)

-It may produce perceptions that the superintendent is a bureaucrat, a perception that may not be readily accepted in this community.

-The superintendent has little knowledge of the power each administrator has in the community. Demanding that they be supportive of the decision may backfire.

-The superintendent may generate the perception that she does not care to listen to others.

3. *If you were a principal in this district, what position would you take? Would it matter if you were an elementary, middle, or high school principal?* In responding to this question, students ought to realize that a decision can be affected by a range of variables. Organizational conditions, environmental conditions, and individual beliefs and values are examples of such variables. For example, it is likely that secondary principals will defend and protect athletic programs.

4. *What is your assessment of the fact that Dr. Marcum knew nothing about financial difficulties until assuming the superintendency?* In pursuing administrative positions, candidates are often preoccupied with personal interests and opportunities. Where this occurs, the administrator is likely to be negligent in assessing the total condition of the position. This seems to have occurred in this case. Dr. Marcum failed to probe the existing weaknesses of the district. This oversight results in surprises once she assumes the superintendency. This should serve as a lesson to students. It is advantageous to learn as much as possible about a

47

position before agreeing to accept it. A candidate should not permit the reputation of the school district or the attractiveness of the position (e.g., status, money) to prevent an indepth analysis of the job opportunity.

5. *In what ways does the community environment make this case somewhat unique?* The information in the case at least suggests that community involvement is rather high. Given this likelihood, many students are apt to believe that the superintendent needs to be very sensitive regarding community reactions. Too often administrators underestimate the potency of political variables in making key decisions. Every decision is in some sense unique, thus the relevance of the community factor in this case should be illuminated. This is a community of well-educated citizens that places a high priority on its public schools. Many citizens may be offended if a new superintendent makes a decision without providing them with an opportunity for input.

6. *Is it important that one of the school board members was a leader in passing petitions to intitiate the strings program?* The fact that a board member was involved in distributing the petitions is important. If nothing else, it tells us that at least one member of the board has a commitment that may prevent her from supporting any decision that does not add a strings teacher.

7. *In your opinion, what would occur if the superintendent decided to initiate the strings program but not add the second counselor?* This decision might well be difficult to explain to the teachers. Teachers may interpret such action as a political move. The teachers may also argue that a second counselor is more important, that is, the position will touch more students and/or provide a more needed service.

8. *Give your assessment of each of the administrators based on what is presented in this case. If you were a superintendent, would you want these individuals on your staff? Why or why not?* Although there are several different positions taken by the administrators in this case, the responses can be divided into two basic groups: (1) those who are willing to take a position, and (2) those who are willing to let the superintendent make the decision. Leaders differ in their expectations of subordinates. Some students

in your class may prefer to work with subordinates who are blindly obedient. Others will opt for administrative staff members who are willing to state and defend their beliefs. You may have some difficulty getting students to give candid responses to this question. Interjecting material regarding leadership styles to exhibit the advantages and disadvantages of two alternatives is helpful. Material from Yukl (1989; see reading list at the end of this case) is especially useful in this regard.

9. *Given that this issue is being confronted during the first six weeks of the superintendent's tenure in the district, does the case have any special significance?* Many individuals will develop perceptions of the new superintendent based on behaviors observed in the early months in the position. In some organizational cultures, it may be extremely difficult to alter these perceptions over time even if they are erroneous. Therefore, a superintendent should be conscious of how all segments of the organization (school district) and the environment (community) interpret decisions made in the first few months on the job. There are two dimensions in this case that deserve special mention in this regard: (1) whether the superintendent will be perceived as sensitive to political pressures (i.e., parental pressures, teacher-generated pressures), and (2) whether the superintendent will be perceived as a thoughtful individual who carefully considers information before acting.

10. *In your opinion, does Dr. Marcum have any advantages over her predecessor in addressing the financial woes of the district?* Often school administrators refer to the first six to twelve months of a superintendent's tenure as the "honeymoon" period. This is the belief that in the early portion of a superintendent's tenure, certain latitudes in leadership will be allowed. Accordingly, some will surmise that a new superintendent is in the best position to make the budget cuts. For the person in the job, however, there are other considerations that should be weighed:

    a. Dr. Marcum is replacing a superintendent who had a long tenure in the district. Any decision she makes is likely to result in a comparison between what she did and speculation as to what the previous superintendent would have done.

    b. The departing superintendent is retiring without any indication of conflict between the superintendent and school

49

board. If Dr. Marcum starts off by dividing the school board, this may not be perceived positively in the community.

c. There is a gender change in the superintendency. The case does not tell us whether Dr. Marcum is the first female superintendent in the district, which may be important. Making unpopular decisions early in her tenure may bring certain prejudices to the surface.

d. Given the level of education in this community, it is likely that citizens will be less willing to take for granted that the superintendent is always correct in making critical decisions, that is, the community is more likely to reject legitimate or expert power with regard to unpopular decisions.

These and other related conditions suggest that the "honeymoon" effect could be less pronounced in this case than would be true in most circumstances. Yet the new superintendent does have some distinct advantages because she has been in her position only a short period of time. She could, for example, claim objectivity, noting that she was not associated with past decisions that contributed to the present financial condition.

OTHER SUGGESTED ACTIVITIES

1. Have your students identify the mechanisms used in local school districts to develop budgets. In particular, see if they can determine the extent to which building level administrators are involved in the process. You may wish to discuss the concept of school-site budgeting.

2. Participatory decision making is another topic that is prominent in our professional literature. Discuss the advantages and disadvantages of the superintendent seeking input from her administrative staff. The work of Vroom and Jago (1988; see reading list at the end of this case) will be especially helpful in this regard.

3. Have your students examine research and theories related to gender differences in leadership. Do these sources produce any insight that is useful to this case? There are a number of doctoral dissertations that have been completed since the mid 1970s that are

50

useful in this regard (e.g., C. B. Jackson - University of Colorado, 1980; A.S. McNutt - Peabody College of Vanderbilt University, 1979).

SUGGESTED READINGS:

Belasco, J., & Alutto, J. (1972). Decisional participation and teacher satisfaction. *Educational Administration Quarterly*, 8(1), 44-58.*

Benson, N., & Malone, P. (1987). Teacher beliefs about shared decision making and work alienation. *Education*, 107, 244-251.

Cibulka, J. (1987). Theories of education budgeting: Lessons from management of decline. *Educational Administration Quarterly*, 23(4), 7-40.

Estler, S. (1988). Decision making. In N. Boyan (Ed.), *Handbook of research on educational administration*, pp. 321-340. White Plains, NY: Longman.*

Gittell, M. (1980). *Limits to citizen participation: The decline of community organization*. Beverly Hills, CA: Sage Publications.*

Grandori, A. (1984). A prescriptive contingency view of organizational decision making. *Administrative Science Quarterly*, 29, 192-208.

Guthrie, J., & Reed, R. (1986). *Educational administration and policy*, pp. 241-245. Englewood Cliffs, NJ: Prentice-Hall.

Hoy, W., & Miskel, C. (1987). *Educational administration: Theory, research and practice* (3rd ed.), pp. 332-350. New York: Random House.

Jackson, C. (1980). *Career development for women in public school administration: A study of women school superintendents in the United States*. Unpublished Ph.D. thesis, University of Colorado, Boulder.*

Lakowski, G. (1987). Values and decision making in educational administration. *Educational Administration Quarterly*, 23(4), 70-82.

Locke, E., & Schweiger, D. (1979). Participation in decision making: One more look. *Research on Organizational Behavior*, 1, 265-339.*

Lowe, R., & Gervails, R. (1987). How to handle desperation budget cuts without despair. *Executive Educator*, 9(1), 18-19.

Lyons, J. (1987). A study of public school principals' decision-making authority and autonomy. *Contemporary Education*, 58(4), 197-200.

McNutt, A. (1979). *A study of the role modes of top echelon women administrators in southern public institutions of higher education.* Unpublished Ph.D. thesis, Peabody College of Vanderbilt University.*

Ornstein, A. (1989). Trimming the fat, stretching the meat for 1990s budgets. *The School Administrator*, 9(46), 20-21.

Owens, R., & Lewis, E. (1976). Managing participation in organizational decisions. *Group and Organizational Studies*, 1, 55-56.

Pajak, E. (1989). *The central office supervisor of curriculum and instruction*, chap. 12. Boston: Allyn & Bacon.

Parker, S. (1984). Cutting school budgets: Dangers and opportunities. *Contemporary Education*, 55(3), 160-163.

Poster, J. (1987). *The limits of consensus.* ERIC, Document Number ED280189.

Roetter, P. (1987). *Decision making style: Does it make a difference?* Unpublished Ph.D. thesis, University of Michigan, Ann Arbor.

Vroom, V., & Jago, A. (1988). *The new leadership: Managing participation in organizations.* Englewood Cliffs, NJ: Prentice-Hall.*

Yukl, G. (1989). *Leadership in organizations* (2nd ed.). Englewood Cliffs, NJ: Prentice-Hall.*

*readings not included in the text

CASE 7

USING COMMITTEES TO MAKE KEY DECISIONS

BACKGROUND INFORMATION

This case focuses on an increasingly common occurrence--a school system that has traditionally employed superintendents from within the school system deciding that the time has come to employ a chief executive from outside the organization. Often the decision to bring in an "outsider" is prompted by a change of school board members and/or a change in school board philosophy. Given that employees become accustomed to established organizational practices, this decision usually creates anxiety among the administrative staff. Principals and central office personnel often observe every action, every decision of the new leader seeking clues to administrative style, biases, and so forth.

The disagreement over petty cash funds in this case exemplifies how one administrator tries to use the change in leadership to advance an unpopular initiative. Would the assistant superintendent have pushed this matter if the new superintendent was a person who was already in the district? This case illustrates the type of challenges and questions that are laid at the doorstep of a new superintendent, especially a superintendent who is still unfamiliar with the culture of the organization.

THE CHALLENGE

Students basically have two choices in responding to the challenge: (1) move forward with the ad hoc committee, ignoring the pleas of the two assistant superintendents, or (2) rescind the decision of using an ad hoc committee. Students who opt not to move forward with the committee may be influenced by: (1) the traditional (bureaucratic) position that preserves the sanctity of organizational divisions (i.e., essentially the position of the assistant superintendent for business), or (2) the political perspective that places importance on the majority view (i.e., essentially the position of the assistant superintendent for instruction). Students who opt to use the ad hoc

53

committee despite staff protests usually justify such action for two reasons: (1) they believe the superintendent needs to follow personal convictions, and (2) they believe that acquiescing to staff wishes will be viewed as a sign of weakness.

Regardless of the position taken, students should be asked to provide information regarding the factors influencing their decision and the sources of these factors (e.g., research, theory, practice, common sense). As with all of the cases, it is critically important that you gain insight into the student's decision-making tendencies. Does the student react on impulse, rely on experience, use acquired information, and so forth?

KEY ISSUES/QUESTIONS

1. *Identify the range of options available to the superintendent at this point. What are the advantages and disadvantages of each?* Some options include:

   a. Staying with the original decision to use an ad hoc committee as constituted.

   b. Staying with the original decision to use an ad hoc committee but appointing more administrators to the committee.

   c. Rescinding the decision to use an ad hoc committee and opting for an alternative that appears to be more acceptable to the two assistant superintendents (e.g., having them co-chair a study committee).

   d. Deciding not to do the study and continuing to permit the petty cash until they are legally challenged.

   e. Deciding not to do the study and to discontinue the petty cash funds.

   f. Involving the school board and letting them advise him on what he should do.

You may want to assign students the task of identifying advantages and disadvantages of each of these options as an out-of-class assignment.

2. *Why do you think the assistant superintendents reacted so strongly in this matter? Do you believe that the organizational climate has anything to do with their reactions?* It is highly possible that the assistant superintendents are accustomed to having their own

domains of power within the organization. The issue of petty cash funds becomes the first real test of whether the new superintendent will respect these divisions of authority. In this case, the superintendent exhibits a desire for objectivity. He also makes a critical statement with regard to his personal philosophy when he suggests that all citizens are stakeholders in the school district. When "turf" battles occur within organizations, it is not surprising that subordinates (in this case principals) loyally support their supervisor.

3. *Some administrators might argue that Dr. Quillen should have attempted to reach a compromise between the two assistant superintendents so that they could have presented a united front to the principals. Do you agree that this would have been a better alternative than the one he pursued? Why or why not?* Politically, it would be advantageous for the superintendent to move forward on this item with the support of both of his assistant superintendents. Students should weigh this consideration against two other variables deemed important by the superintendent: (1) objectivity in reaching a solution, (2) acknowledging a range of stakeholders in the decision. The values and beliefs of the participants in this case become extremely important in assessing the political dimensions of the problem. You should point out that leaders frequently encounter conflict between political and professional issues.

4. *Are ad hoc committees effective? What are the strengths and weaknesses of this approach to dealing with problems?* Have your students develop information about the use of committees in school systems. Some people criticize ad hoc committees because the members usually accept little responsibility for the consequences of their recommendations. Once their task is completed, they disband and are not held responsible for the consequences. By contrast, committees can provide a broad range of support for a difficult decision. Committees represent a democratic form of reaching consensus. Finally, committees often bring together individuals who possesses varying knowledge and perspectives. Such diversity may contribute to more effective recommendations.

5. *Do you believe that the issue in question is serious enough for the superintendent to risk his working relationships with his top two assistants?* Many experienced superintendents believe that you must

choose battles carefully. That is, high conflict situations often require the leader to expend energy and power. Thus, knowing which issues are of greatest importance is deemed critical. Whether or not this issue will be identified as important enough to risk relationships with the top two assistants is a matter of personal perception. First of all, there is not sufficient information provided in this case to determine what other issues are facing the superintendent. In addition, the fact that the superintendent is new in the district (and replacing a person who held the job for eighteen years) is not inconsequential. Although the matter of petty cash funds alone may not be that critical, when considered in the context of communicating leadership values and beliefs it becomes a more weighty consideration.

6. *Identify some steps the superintendent can take to assure the board and professional staff that his idea of an ad hoc committee can work.* Anytime a leader moves forward with an initiative that is controversial, it is advantageous to explicate the perceived problem, the process to be used in addressing the problem, and the expected outcomes. The school board and the administrative staff may be more supportive if they understand the superintendent's motivations and expectations in establishing the committee. The superintendent should not expect that all members of the school community will continually be influenced by legitimate authority. Explaining the underpinnings of a critical decision may not change the minds of individuals, but it will project an image of a leader who thinks that members of the organization have a right to know why certain initiatives are being followed. The superintendent could use examples of comparable situations to exhibit why he thinks his decision on this matter will be effective.

7. *If you were a principal in this district, how would you interpret the superintendent's decision to use a committee? Does this decision provide insight into the new superintendent's leadership style?* A variety of answers can be expected. Many students will view the superintendent as a person of principle, that is, they will see him as more interested in democratic processes than in building political power. Other students are likely to view the superintendent as politically naive. They will assess his behavior as being too risky. As mentioned previously, there are two strong cues in this case as to what the superintendent views as being important--objectivity and

participatory decision making. By not siding with either assistant superintendent, the superintendent may be purposefully transmitting the message that he is independent. He may want administrative staff to believe that he will make every decision based on the merits of the evidence and not political linkages. He also may be purposefully avoiding a situation where he identifies one major division of the school district as being more important than another.

8. *Discuss the concept of project management. Does it have any relevance to this case?* Project management attempts to utilize the assets of the organization to solve a problem without concern for traditional boundaries found in bureaucracies. Thus, committees may be composed of individuals from varying divisions of the organization and individuals possessing different skills and knowledge. By contrast, bureaucratic organizations tend to assign research or problem-solving tasks to the specific division of the organization having jurisdiction over the area being examined, for example, business affairs studies an issue related to finances. By creating this ad hoc committee, the superintendent is utilizing some elements of project management. Although the two parents possess expertise associated with the study, that is not necessarily true of the remaining members of the committee. In private industry, the project method is often based entirely on expertise. Here it appears more on a combination of expertise and school-community representation.

9. *In the early 1960s, research focusing on career bound versus place bound administrators emerged in the literature. Does this research have any value in analyzing behaviors in this case?* Research on career bound and place bound administrators indicates that a career bound administrator's behavior is influenced by a specific career goal (e.g., becoming a superintendent). By contrast, place bound administrators are more interested in maintaining their current jobs, employer, and so forth. One could suggest that on the basis of mobility, this case brings together a career bound superintendent with a place bound staff. The work of R. Carlson (1961, 1972; see reading list at the end of this case) is especially cogent to this aspect of the case.

57

OTHER SUGGESTED ACTIVITIES

1. Have students discuss the potential implications for a school district located in an area where there is a growing number of retirees coupled with a declining student population.

2. Discuss the importance of this school district being in a county where retirees are locating while other counties in the state are openly pursuing industrial development.

3. Invite one or more experienced superintendents to your class to discuss the importance of the first months on the job with respect to employee perceptions of leadership style.

SUGGESTED READINGS:

Black, J., & English, F. (1986). *What they don't tell you in schools of education about school administration,* chap. 1. Lancaster, PA: Technomic.

Byers, G. (1984). *Training school staffs in concepts of participatory management in the Fairfax County Public Schools An evaluation study.* Unpublished Ed.D. thesis, Virginia Polytechnic Institute and State University.

Carlson, R. (1961). Succession and performance among school superintendents. *Administrative Science Quarterly, 6,* 210-227.

Carlson, R. (1972). *School superintendents: Careers and performance.* Columbus, OH: Charles Merrill.*

Crowson, R. (1987). The local school district superintendency: A puzzling role. *Educational Administration Quarterly, 23(4),* 49-69.

Greenhalgh, J. (1978). *Practitioner's guide to school business management,* chap. 2. Boston: Allyn & Bacon.

Hamner, T., & Turk, J. (1987). Organizational determinants of leader behavior and authority. *Journal of Applied Psychology, 72,* 647-682.*

Hanson, E. (1985). *Educational administration and organizational behavior* (2nd ed.), pp. 294-306. Boston: Allyn & Bacon.

Hughes, L., & Ubben, G. (1984). *The elementary principal's handbook* (2nd ed.), pp. 304-309. Boston: Allyn & Bacon.

Lakowski, G. (1987). Values and decision making in educational administration. *Educational Administration Quarterly*, 23(4), 70-82.

Meadows, B. (1990). The rewards and risks of shared leadership. *Phi Delta Kappan*, 71, 545-548.*

McInerney, W. (1985). Participation in educational planning at the school district level. *Planning and Changing*, 16, 206-215.

Miklos, E. (1988). Administrator selection, career patterns, succession, and socialization. In N. Boyan (Ed.) *Handbook of research on educational administration*, pp. 53-76. White Plains, NY: Longman.

Owens, R., & Lewis, E. (1976). Managing participation in organizational decisions. *Group and Organizational Studies*, 1, 55-56.

Pajak, E. (1989). *The central office supervisor of curriculum and instruction*, chap. 8. Boston: Allyn & Bacon.

Pitner, N., & Ogawa, R. (1981). Organizational leadership: The case of the school superintendent. *Educational Administration Quarterly*, 17(2), 45-65.*

Roetter, P. (1987). *Decision making style: Does it make a difference*. Unpublished Ph.D. thesis, University of Michigan, Ann Arbor.

Watson, P. (1986). Effective task forces: Getting a quality product in minimum time. *Planning and Changing*, 17, 131-145.

Yukl, G. (1989). *Leadership in organizations* (2nd ed.), chap. 3. Englewood Cliffs, NJ: Prentice-Hall.

*readings not included in the text

CASE 8

AN EFFORT TO STUDY SCHOOL-BASED MANAGEMENT

BACKGROUND INFORMATION

This case takes place in a rather small city where there is a sharp division in socioeconomic status among taxpayers. The school board composition is constantly changing as incumbents find it difficult to retain their seats. At least in part, instability on the board spawns frequent turnovers in the superintendency. When the more affluent community members gain control of four of the five seats on the board, they decide it is time to employ a change-oriented superintendent and move forward with long-range planning.

The new chief executive has many years of administrative experience, but not as a superintendent. He spends his first six months in the position attempting to diagnose the difficulties that have plagued the district in the past. He decides that more taxpayers must be allowed to participate in the governance of the district and he determines that school-based management may be the means for achieving this goal. His decision to move forward in recommending a feasibility study to examine the advantages and disadvantages of school-based management are immediately challenged by his administrative staff.

The superintendent is faced with several potential problems. Does he move forward with what he thinks is necessary regardless of how it affects the morale and perceptions of his administrative staff? Does he take advantage of the current board support to initiate changes? Does he decide to compromise (e.g., move more slowly and try to change the attitudes of his administrative staff)?

THE CHALLENGE

This case evolves to a point where the superintendent is faced with problems no matter what he decides to do. Consider the following possibilities:

1. He ignores the petition from his administrators and makes his recommendation to the board but does not take any action against the high school principal or other administrators.

2. He ignores the petition and makes his recommendation to the board but either reprimands or recommends the removal of the high school principal.

3. He decides that he is moving too quickly and agrees to delay making his recommendation until he has more time to discuss the matter with his administrative staff.

4. He decides not to recommend the study and to look at other alternatives to creating community participation (alternatives that may be more acceptable to his administrative staff).

5. He seeks the counsel of the school board members indicating that he is willing to delay or abandon the recommendation if they advise him to do so.

6. He decides to delay making the recommendation until he is able to gather information relative to how teachers and parents react to the potentiality of moving to school-based management.

Have the students identify perceived advantages and disadvantages for each of these options.

KEY ISSUES/QUESTIONS

1. *Assess the judgments the superintendent is making about the nature of the community and the relationship between a socioeconomic polarization and problems in the school district.* At least on the basis of the information presented in this case, it is quite possible that the superintendent's assessments are correct. With the sharp division in the community along socioeconomic lines, it is highly likely that significantly different educational philosophies exist in the north and south parts of the city. These differences are expressed in school board elections and the poor retention rates for superintendents. The potential negative effects on the school district are obvious; for example, rapid turnover in the superintendency

makes long-range planning virtually impossible. It is possible that the superintendent may be wrong in connecting the community polarization to the school district's problems, but nothing in the case would support this conclusion.

2. *Was it appropriate for Dr. Hollman to talk Dr. Pisak into applying for the superintendency in Lewis?* Increasingly, school districts are turning to consultants to provide assistance in filling key vacancies. This is a practice that has been more prevalent in higher education and private business than it has in public schools. Consultants realize that their reputation among school districts rests with getting good applicant pools. The school should expect that the consultant will seek out the best candidates, especially those who might otherwise not apply. This is one reason they are paying him a fee. The information in this case does not suggest that there was excessive "arm twisting." It appears that Dr. Pisak had confidence in his former mentor and decided to follow his advice. One could argue that Dr. Pisak could have withdrawn after either the first or second interview if he did not want the job. The consultant merely encouraged him to apply.

3. *Should Dr. Pisak have asked the principals their opinion if there was a chance he would ignore what they said?* The superintendent appears to have been seeking input. The case does not suggest he was holding a referendum on the issue. Often groups perceive that when they are asked to render an opinion or a recommendation that they are, de facto, making a decision. Knowing the majority of your staff does not support an initiative is important; but most seasoned administrators would argue that this one piece of information must be weighed against other factors. In a district characterized by intense political activity by school board members, it is reasonable for administrators to expect problems to be handled primarily from a political perspective.

4. *Identify the strengths and weaknesses of school-based management.* Practitioners disagree on the value of school-based management. Some contend it is the most appropriate alternative for democratic governance. Supporters also note that it builds community support and results in better communications among groups within the school/community. Detractors view it as a boondoggle. They argue that each school will become a mini-school

system.   A host of legal and educational problems could result if each school is permitted to pursue its own course.   Furthermore, critics see school-based management as a spawning ground for conflict.   There is also the concern that teachers, not parents, will become the dominant force on school councils.   This is an area where students should be encouraged to pursue additional readings. Information on school-based management will evolve throughout the 1990s as more school districts decide to experiment with the process. You may want to assign students the task of looking for information detailing the successes and failures of the process.

5. *To what extent do environmental conditions (community) and organizational climate affect the implementation of school-based management?*   School districts that have traditionally had a high concentration of power at the school board/superintendent level or at the principal level are apt to have difficulty allowing school councils to make critical decisions.   The potency of the local teachers' union is another factor that may affect acceptance.   The American Federation of Teachers has been supportive of school-based management, especially in situations where the local school councils are given a broad range of authority.   School districts that have been rather stable and possess low levels of conflict may react negatively to the process if it produces bickering and inefficiency in reaching decisions.   The community and school district climate are indeed critical factors in determining the probable success of school-based management.

6. *Evaluate the behavior of the high school principal in this matter. Do you believe the rapid turnover rate of superintendents in the district affected his behavior?*   The direct challenge of the superintendent's program made by the high school principal could be attributed to several factors   individual personality is one; the leadership style of the principal is another.   It is highly possible that the rapid turnover of superintendents has created a perception among the administrative staff that the person occupying this position has limited power.   Past practices in the school system may be yet another factor to consider.   The high school principal's behavior also may be affected by his knowledge that this is a somewhat stressful situation for the new superintendent.   Dr. Pisak has never been a superintendent before; he is in a community environment that is relatively new to him; and he is functioning in an organization that

has been unstable for the past decade. All of these conditions make him somewhat vulnerable to challenges from his subordinates. The information provided in the case is insufficient to draw definite conclusions about the factors motivating and directing the high school principal's behavior. Nevertheless, you should point out the value of considering the possibilities enumerated here. Weighing these possibilities, especially in the context of leadership theories, permits students to make more enlightened responses to the challenge.

7. *Should the superintendent have had more discussions with the board and administration before deciding to recommend the feasibility study?* The case suggests that the administrators were surprised by the superintendent's decision to move forward quickly, even after a majority of them recommended against the study. You may want your students to develop a list of perceived advantages and disadvantages of the superintendent's actions. For example, one could argue that individuals who are opposed to the concept of school-based management would use additional discussions to try to scuttle the feasibility study. On the other hand, one could contend that added discussions would have allowed the superintendent to explicate his perceptions, biases, or why he chose not to listen to his staff. Should Dr. Pisak have taken the time to explain to his staff and the school board why he asked for opinions? Maybe he should have been more emphatic in noting that he was simply seeking advice. Another dimension of this question relates to possible impressions that may be drawn by the staff of the superintendent (e.g., he is an impulsive individual; he is insensitive to staff opinions).

8. *If you were a principal in this school district, would you have signed the petition to the superintendent? Why or why not?* It is likely that students in your class will be divided on this issue. Several may even be unable to answer the question. This question is valuable because it permits you to probe the values, beliefs, and perceptions motivating one to either sign or not sign a petition. Students who say they would not sign the petition should be questioned as to how they would handle peer reactions (i.e., coping with the possible negative reactions from other principals). Also, ask your students if the petition will influence the board to not approve the study. The students should understand that either course

of action, signing or not signing the petition, can create personal problems.

9. *Are there any conditions in the community and school district that suggest the superintendent was correct in moving quickly to recommend a feasibility study?* Dr. Pisak seems to be motivated by his conclusion that organizational instability, especially on the school board and in the superintendency, has been caused by socioeconomic polarization in the community. He sees school-based management as one possibility for reducing the negative effects of this condition. If one considers the short tenure of Dr. Pisak's predecessors, it may be reasonable to move forward with the study as soon as possible. Often such studies are time consuming and the results may be debated for months after the study is concluded. Thus, the superintendent has to weigh time parameters as they affect this issue.

Discuss the importance of time in reaching critical decisions. Many students are prone to be cautious; accordingly, they overlook problems associated with delays in making decisions. This case offers another opportunity to discuss risk taking in relationship to organizational and environmental turmoil. Given the instability within the school system over the past decade, high risk behavior may be appropriate to achieve change.

10. *Given the information in this case, how do you believe the board will react if: (a) the superintendent moves forward with his recommendation in spite of the petition, or (b) he decides to withdraw the recommendation because of the petition?* Given the conditions under which Dr. Pisak was employed, it is likely that a majority of the school board will be supportive of his recommendation. There are clear indications from the information provided in the case that the majority seeks change and reform. For the new superintendent to back down because his administrative staff disagrees with conducting the study could cause some school board members to wonder if they hired the right person for the job. You can inject the topic of reflective practice to exhibit how the superintendent could benefit from weighing the myriad factors associated with this case.

OTHER SUGGESTED ACTIVITIES

1. Discuss the purpose of feasibility studies. If possible, bring examples of such studies to class and discuss the outcomes.

2. Invite two practitioners with opposing views on school-based management to your class.

3. Discuss ways a candidate for a superintendency can weigh conditions in a community and school district prior to accepting a position. Relate this discussion to the superintendent in this case.

4. Identify the positions of the National Education Association (NEA) and American Federation of Teachers (AFT) regarding school-based management.

5. Have your students evaluate the statements included in the petition signed by the nine principals.

6. Discuss the advantages and disadvantages of the superintendent recommending the dismissal of the high school principal.

SUGGESTED READINGS:

Beaudette, D. (1987). *School based management: A typology and analysis of practices in two New Hampshire school districts.* Unpublished Ed.D. thesis, Boston University.

Bell, J. (1986). *A study of the relationship between community participation in educational governance and the socio-political environment of the school board.* Unpublished Ed.D. thesis, Virginia Polytechnic Institute and State University.*

Black, J., & English, F. (1986). *What they don't tell you in schools of education about school administration,* pp. 15-17. Lancaster, PA: Technomics.

Caldwell, S., & Wood, F. (1988). School-based improvement -- Are we ready? *Educational Leadership,* 46(2), 50-53.

Cawelti, G. (1989). Key elements of site-based management. *Educational Leadership,* 46(8), 46.

Chapman, J. (1988). A new conception of the principalship: Decentralization, devolution, and the administration of Australian schools. In D. Griffiths, R. Stout, & P. Forsyth (Eds.), *Leaders for American schools*, pp. 429-438. Berkeley, CA: McCutchan.

Clark, E. (1985). *Motivations of participants in school community councils as related to the characteristics of participants, councils and schools.* Unpublished Ed.D. thesis, University of Southern California.*

Conley, S., & Bacharach, S. (1990). From school-site management to participatory school-site management. *Phi Delta Kappan*, 71, 549-552.*

David, J. (1989). Synthesis of Research on School-Based Management. *Educational Leadership*, 46(8), 45-53.

Drucker, P. (1980). *Managing in turbulent times.* New York: Harper & Row.*

Fink, J. (1987). *A description of community involvement in high schools identified as exemplary by the National Commission on Excellence in Education.* Unpublished Ph.D. thesis, Miami University.*

Guthrie, J. (1986). School based management: The next needed education reform. *Phi Delta Kappan*, 68(4), 305-309.

Guthrie, J., & Reed, R. (1986). *Educational administration and policy,* pp. 16-18. Englewood Cliffs, NJ: Prentice-Hall.

Hanson, E. (1985). *Educational administration and organizational behavior* (2nd ed.), pp. 76-78; 103-109. Boston: Allyn & Bacon.

Harrison, C. (1989). Site-based management: The realities of implementation. *Educational Leadership*, 46(8), 55-58.*

Hoy, W., & Forsyth, P. (1986). *Effective supervision: Theory into practice*, pp. 168-177. New York: Random House.

Kowalski, T. (1986). The second coming of community education. *Contemporary Education,* 57(4), 194-197. (also in *Education Digest*, 52(6), 52-54)

Kowalski, T., & Fallon, J. (1986). *Community education: Processes and programs.* Fastback 243. Bloomington, IN: Phi Delta Kappa Educational Foundation.

Lawler, E. (1986). *High involvement management,* chap. 1. San Francisco, CA: Jossey-Bass.

Lewis, A. (1989). *Restructuring American schools*, chap. 9. Arlington, VA: American Association of School Administrators.

McWalters, P. (1988). New realities call for new rules. *The School Administrator*, 45(8), 13-15.

Murphy, J. (1989). The paradox of decentralizing schools: Lessons from government, and the Catholic church. *Phi Delta Kappan*, 70(10), 808-812.*

Ratzki, A. (1988). Creating a school community: One model of how it can be done. *American Educator: The Professional Journal of the American Federation of Teachers*, 12(1), 10-17, 38-43.

Scarr, L. (1988). Lake Washington master plan: A system for growth. *Educational Leadership*, 46(2), 13-16.

Sergiovanni, T. (1987). *The principalship: A reflective practice perspective*, pp. 323-329. Boston: Allyn & Bacon.

Smith, J. (1985). *School based management*. Unpublished Ed.D. thesis, Harvard University.

Stover, D. (1989). But some principals feel threatened. *Executive Educator*, 11(1), 17.

Wagner, J., & Gooding, R. (1987). Shared influence and organizational behavior: A meta-analysis of situational variables expected to moderate participation-outcome relationships. *Academy of Management Journal*, 30, 524-541.*

Wicks, T., & Pankake, A. (1989-90). Board of education and superintendent: The team that "empowers" effectiveness. *National Forum of Educational Administration and Supervision Journal*, 7(1), 117-123.

Yukl, G. (1989). *Leadership in organizations* (2nd ed.), pp. 112-119. Englewood Cliffs, NJ: Prentice-Hall.

Zerchykov, R. (1985). Why school councils? *Equity and Choice*, 2(1), 37-38.

*not included in the text

CASE 9

INVOLVING TEACHERS IN EMPLOYMENT DECISIONS

BACKGROUND INFORMATION

Relatively inexperienced practitioners are especially vulnerable to believing that the effectiveness of administrative actions is universal. In Case 9, a principal decides to utilize an employment process she experienced while working as an assistant principal in a university-based laboratory school. This process, involving teachers in the employment interviews, is utilized by some school districts but continues to be prohibited in many others. The principal in this case seems to ignore: (1) past practices in the district, and (2) the implications of teacher involvement in employment interviews for collective bargaining.

The changing nature of the community is reflected in the school system's willingness to seek administrators from outside of the district. Interestingly, the two key figures in this case are females who are relatively new residents in the community. This fact will raise questions relative to whether the superintendent would have reacted the same if the principal was a male or an employee with a long tenure in the school district. Changing values and beliefs about leadership often spawn conflict as the "old" and "new" ideas come face to face. On the one hand, the school leadership embraces decentralization in employment practices; yet, the superintendent clings to the notion that employment must be preserved as strictly an administrative function.

THE CHALLENGE

Individuals react very differently to reprimands. Some principals are able to shrug off such action whereas others may be totally demoralized. The letter of reprimand is especially complex in this case because it is given to a principal who appears to be performing at a very satisfactory level with regard to most responsibilities.

Students should be encouraged to justify the position they take and to identify the range of alternatives they considered. The following are some of the more obvious:

1. Ignore the reprimand and continue to do what you think is best.

2. Attempt to discuss the matter with your supervisor so that a greater exchange of views and information is possible.

3. Turn to the teachers for support.

4. Challenge the reprimand by either asking to appear before the school board on the matter or requesting that you be allowed to have a written response placed in your personnel file.

5. Accept the reprimand but commit yourself to changing the system, that is, getting the school district to permit teachers to be involved in employment interviews.

6. Resign from the school district.

A key element of the challenge is whether the principal would discontinue the practice of including teachers in employment interviews. The reprimand does not state that the principal is prohibited from continuing this practice. Rather, the letter rebukes her for not properly communicating with her supervisor and for not obtaining permission to include faculty in the interviews. If the principal decides not to involve faculty in the future, the faculty may react very negatively. If the principal decides to continue the practice, the difficulties with the central office are likely to intensify. Given the circumstances, the principal may find it necessary to reach some type of compromise position. For instance, is it possible to include the teachers in some fashion that will be acceptable to the superintendent? This question should be raised with the students.

KEY ISSUES/QUESTIONS

1. *What options does Dr. White have at this point?* The primary options are identified in the discussion of the challenge. One additional option is to seek legal counsel. This course of action is

especially true if the principal decides to formally challenge the school district. In practice, many administrators simply accept reprimands. Engage your students in a conversation regarding why administrators often choose not to challenge such actions. You may wish to discuss the merits and pitfalls of reprimands. Are they effective in changing leadership behavior?

2. *What alternatives could have been pursued by the superintendent and/or the assistant superintendent for instruction in dealing with this issue?* By issuing a formal, written reprimand, the superintendent created a difficult situation. If the teachers find out that their principal has been reprimanded, they may decide to publicize the matter. If the principal decides to abruptly halt the practice, then she may destroy rapport with her faculty. It may have been more effective to attempt adjudication through private discussions. Such discussions would have permitted both sides to state their views and to work toward a mutually acceptable solution. Nowhere in this case does it state that the school district has a policy prohibiting the participation of faculty in employment interviews. For this reason alone, many observers may view the reprimand as being unduly harsh.

3. *Identify conditions in the community that you believe are cogent to this case.* Some of the more cogent considerations include the following:
   a. The community was changing from a predominately rural area to a more heterogeneous population base. Many of the new residents were not farmers.
   b. Education probably plays a key role in community life given the presence of the public community college and private liberal arts college.
   c. The diversity of occupations on the school board is reflective of the community at large. For instance, the case indicates that changes in the district may stem from board initiatives, not the leadership of the superintendent, (e.g., the curtailment of internal promotions).

These factors are important because they provide clues relative to the environmental field of the school district. New residents are likely to bring new ideas and expectations. The results of this change can be unsettling for the school district leadership. Administrators

71

are usually threatened when long-standing practices are questioned. Overall, the case portrays a community in transition.

4. *Identify conditions in the school district that you believe are cogent to this case.* The following conditions deserve mention:
    a. The superintendent worked his way to the top position by receiving an internal promotion (he was high school principal prior to becoming the superintendent).
    b. In recent years, there has been a willingness to employ administrators from other school districts and geographic locations.
    c. The line relationships within the district reflect a rather traditional organization. The principals report to an assistant superintendent rather than to the superintendent.
    d. The superintendent delegates authority but expects subordinates to answer for their decisions.
    e. The school district administration is a mix of persons who have been promoted through the ranks within the district and "outsiders." It is noteworthy that both key figures in this case are females who did not reach their positions by internal promotions and who both hold doctorates.
    f. Three of the unsuccessful candidates for the high school principalship are administrators in the district.

Administrators in organizations that historically promote leaders internally often find it difficult to accept a change in this practice. The controversy in this case may intensify opposition among some administrators and board members regarding the employment of "outsiders."

5. *Do you believe that the assistant superintendent for instruction should be held accountable for the decisions of the high school principal?* The high school principal clearly reports to the assistant superintendent for instruction. The principal is not only new to the school system, she is in her first year as principal. It seems reasonable that the assistant superintendent should have discussed employment practices with her. Given the potentiality for legal and collective bargaining problems related to employment practices, school districts ought to provide staff development, manuals, and supervision for the process. This did not occur. One could argue that the superintendent and assistant superintendent were negligent.

On the other hand, it is also reasonable to expect that a new principal would investigate employment practices, ask questions, and the like before proceeding with teacher selection.

6. *Describe what is meant by teacher empowerment. In general, do you agree with the principal's judgment that teacher empowerment is needed? Why or why not?* Reform reports throughout the 1980s refer to teacher empowerment. Many educators believe teachers must be given more autonomy to make decisions regarding professional practice. Frequently, advocates for teacher empowerment identify peer selection as one aspect of increasing the decision-making power of practitioners. Administrators accustomed to working in school systems maintaining a centralization of authority often criticize the involvement of faculty in important decisions, citing their perceptions that teachers are not held accountable for the results of those decisions. Two other factors may be associated with opposition to allowing teachers to participate in employment interviews: (1) union-related issues (e.g., fear that the union will control employment decisions), and (2) school board member perceptions that employment is strictly a management function (e.g., board members who embrace management values prevalent in the private sector). Increasingly, school districts are moving toward involving teachers in employment decisions. You may want to identify school systems that have done so in your state or immediate vicinity and detail the procedures used in those instances for your students.

7. *Evaluate the principal's position that she is responsible for employment recommendations and ought to be given the latitude to determine who will be involved in the interviewing process.* One side of this issue relates to the practice of delegating authority. It is arguable that a principal given authorization to make employment recommendations ought to be given the latitude to develop procedures for those decisions--so long as those procedures are not in violation of school board policy. By contrast, one could contend that the high school is not an independent unit. Rather it is a visible part of a larger organization. As such, the behavior of the principal has potential ramifications for all the schools and all the professional employees in the school system. When this case is examined from a systemic perspective, the decisions of the principal become more troublesome. One also needs to examine the principal's acceptance

73

of the faculty promise to keep the issue away from collective bargaining. Do teachers at the high school have the authority to make this commitment or the power to see that it is kept?

8. *Assess the position taken by the two assistant principals in this case.* Keep in mind that the two assistant principals were both unsuccessful candidates for the principalship. The information provided indicates that initially both voiced some concern about teacher involvement, but neither overtly opposed or criticized the process. The assistants are in a delicate situation. Anything that they say or do regarding the principal's behavior may be construed as "sour grapes." Given that they shared their views privately with the principal, it is difficult to be critical of their behavior.

9. *Suppose the principal had received a verbal rather than a written reprimand. Do you believe it would have had the same effect?* Persons react to criticism in different ways. A written reprimand usually is perceived as an act related to summative evaluation. If the superintendent and assistant superintendent for instruction had issued a verbal reprimand, it would have been possible to place the reprimand in the context of formative supervision. The argument for a verbal reprimand can be supported by the following points:

    a. The overall performance of the principal is quite good.

    b. The superintendent and assistant superintendent for instruction should share some of the blame for this problem, that is, neither really provided adequate information to the principal about their objections or concerns.

    c. A verbal discussion is more likely to result in a sharing of viewpoints and a resolution acceptable to all parties.

OTHER SUGGESTED ACTIVITIES

1. Invite staff from your university placement office to your class to discuss issues related to involving teachers in peer employment. Questions regarding confidentiality of credentials, effects on job applicants, and observed strengths and weaknesses should be raised.

2. See if you can locate a master contract between a school district and teacher's union that requires faculty involvement in peer employment decisions.

3. Discuss the importance of a staff development program for newly employed administrators.

SUGGESTED READINGS:

Belasco, J., & Alutto, J. (1972). Decisional participation and teacher satisfaction. *Educational Administration Quarterly*, 8(1), 44-58.

Boyan, N. (1988). Describing and explaining administrative behavior. In N. Boyan (Ed.), *Handbook of research on educational administration,* pp. 77-97. White Plains, NY: Longman.

Bredeson, P. (1983). The secondary school principal's role in personnel screening and selection. *High School Journal*, 67, 6-10.

Bromert, J. (1984). The role and effectiveness of search committees. *AAHE Bulletin*, April, 7-10.

Castetter, W. (1985). *The personnel function in educational administration* (4th ed.), chap. 9. New York: Macmillan.

Conway, J. (1984). The myth, mystery, and mastery of participative decision making in education. *Educational Administration Quarterly*, 20(3), 11-40.

Ellis, T., et al. (1987). *Improving school effectiveness through reform of teacher selection practices and collegial observation of classroom performance.* ERIC, Document Number ED281902.

Gips, C., & Bredeson, P. (1984). *The selection of teachers and principals: A model for faculty participation.* ERIC, Document Number ED251974.*

Lewis, A. (1989). *Restructuring America's schools*, chap. 4. Arlington, VA: American Association of School Administrators.

Macguire, J. (1983). Faculty participation in interviewing teacher candidates. *Clearing House*, 56(7), 330-331.

Maxwell, L. (1987). *Improving the selection of teachers: Research in brief.* ERIC, Document Number ED282850.

McPherson, R., & Crowson, R. (1987). Sources of constraints and opportunities for discretion in the principalship. In J. Lane & H. Waldberg (Eds.), *Effective school leadership: Policy and process*, pp. 129-156. Berkeley, CA: McCutchan.

Neidt, W. (1987). *Factors contributing to teacher satisfaction with shared decision-making.* Unpublished Ph.D. thesis, University of Kansas.*

Owens, R., & Lewis, E. (1976). Managing participation in organizational decisions. *Group and Organizational Studies, 1,* 56-66.

Pigford, A. (1989). How to hire teachers that fit. *The School Administrator, 10*(46), 38, 43.

Scarr, L. (1988). Lake Washington's master plan--A system for growth. *Educational Leadership, 46*(2), 13-16.*

Sergiovanni, T. (1987). *The principalship: A reflective practice perspective,* chap. 3. Boston: Allyn & Bacon.*

Snyder, P. (1985). *Perceptions of the managerial behavior of average and unusually effective high school principals.* Unpublished Ph.D. thesis, Pennsylvania State University.

Snyder, K., & Anderson, R. (1986). *Managing productive schools: Toward an ecology,* chap. 1. Orlando, FL: Academic Press College Division.

Stuckwisch, D. (1986). *Patterns of participative decision-making: A study of high schools that promote decision sharing practices.* Unpublished Ph.D. thesis, Virginia Commonwealth University.

Tracy, S. (1986). *Finding the right person--and collegiality.* ERIC, Document Number EJ334581.

Tursman, C. (1989). Ways to fight teacher burnout: An interview with Ivan Fitzwater. *The School Administrator, 46*(3), 30, 35.

Zirkel, P., & Gluckman, I. (1986). Letters of reprimand: The important questions. *NASSP Bulletin, 70*(491), 99-102.

*readings not included in text

RESTRICTING EMPLOYMENT OPPORTUNITIES

BACKGROUND INFORMATION

Political control in small towns is often shared by a few wealthy or otherwise influential individuals (or families). This case presents such a situation. A long-term board president, who is probably the most influential person in the community, exhibits his intention to keep close watch on the school system. One could surmise that he uses his authority on the school board for political purposes, for example, keeping citizens in the community beholden to him.

The new superintendent is following in the footsteps of an individual who retired from the school district. Change is often more difficult to achieve in such situations. Another key feature in this case is the environmental differences between the superintendent's previous and current positions. Moving from a post with the Bureau of Indian Affairs, a large division of the U. S. Department of the Interior, Victor finds himself in a different political environment in Fort Jason.

The case outlines several problems facing the new superintendent. He is being asked to do something that he is not sure is legal, that is, restrict the announcements of vacancies in the school district. Moreover, the content of the case suggests that the superintendent has some procedural disagreements with the directives being given by the board president. Finally, the superintendent is confronted with the likelihood that the board president wants to make all important future decisions. These conditions spawn serious questions for the superintendent. For example, is he willing to be a passive leader in order to survive in Fort Jason?

THE CHALLENGE

One of the most difficult situations for new superintendents is to find that they are expected to play a passive role. Individuals vary markedly in their willingness to adjust to such expectations. Some accept a passive role simply to accommodate financial or family considerations. Others feel comfortable with this role. By contrast, some react strongly to these situations because they are incongruent with personal values and beliefs. Students are apt to display a variety of responses to this challenge. The likely range of responses is outlined in item 1 under Key Issues/Questions. Students should be required to cite the advantages and disadvantages of the approach they select.

KEY ISSUES/QUESTIONS

1. *What alternatives does the superintendent have in this matter?* The following are among the more obvious choices:
   a. Follow the directives of the board president.
   b. Seek counsel from the school attorney.
   c. Seek counsel from someone other than the school attorney (e.g., state school boards' association; from a professor).
   d. Ignore the board president's directive and insist that the board vote on his recommendation as presented.
   e. Ask the entire school board to discuss the issue.
   f. Demand that the school board establish a policy that restricts employment to residents so that no one can question the superintendent's actions in this matter.
   g. Ask the board to delay announcements regarding the vacancies until the matter can be studied and discussed by the entire board.

2. *What are the advantages and disadvantages of the superintendent simply agreeing to do what the board president desires?* If the superintendent does as he is told, he is likely to receive a favorable response from the board president. The information in the case suggests that the board president prefers a superintendent who will follow rather than lead. If the superintendent ignores the wishes of the board president, he is likely to have problems. The severity of these problems may rest with what the superintendent does in lieu of following the directive. For example, seeking counsel about the legal dimensions of the issue may not cause as great a negative reaction as insisting that the board vote on the original recommendation. The board may not want to go on the record as

restricting employment to current residents; and forcing such a vote could truly anger the president.

3. *What legal issues are raised in this case?* Many states have statutory requirements regarding the advertisement of vacancies. You should have your students determine if such laws exist in your state. Moreover, it would be helpful to examine federal laws. Equal opportunity and civil rights statutes are especially cogent. Although the case material makes no mention of the demographics of the two communities other than size, suppose that Fort Jason is without minority citizens and Grundy (the neighboring community) has a large minority population. Could the directive of the board president be construed as an attempt to prevent minorities from being employed? Additionally, school district policy plays a role in this case. From the nature of the discussion between the superintendent and board president, one can assume the board does not have a policy, at least a written one, restricting searches and/or employment to current residents of the school district. Thus, a verbal agreement between the superintendent and board president may have legal implications as well.

4. *Why do you believe that Jimmy Quince has been president of the school board for so long?* Individuals serve on school boards for varying reasons. This is true regardless of whether they serve one year or twenty years. Many are motivated by a sense of civic duty; others are interested in the schools because of their children; some see election to a school board as a first step in a political career; and still others simply have an axe to grind. From reading the case, one knows that Jimmy Quince is a powerful individual in the community. He may derive personal satisfaction from having influence over the school board. He may see some connections between what occurs in the school district and his financial or political interests. It is also possible that he is a person who has the best of intentions but simply does not understand the role of a school board member. One can only speculate in responding to this question.

5. *What are the advantages and disadvantages of having very little turnover in membership on a school board?* Stability permits a school district to engage in long-range planning. Unfortunately, few districts with stable boards capitalize on this opportunity. Stability also can create effective working relationships (e.g., the

79

superintendent is not required to constantly adjust to new individuals). New school board members usually go through an extensive learning process once they are seated. Sometimes it takes two to three years just to grasp the basic framework of the organization. Accordingly, instability requires the superintendent to expend time to orientate board members to their roles and to the school district. One common problem with instability entails changes in philosophy and goals. Often, new board members will have a "different agenda" than their predecessors. School districts experiencing constant changes in direction find it extremely difficult to implement new ideas. One board may plant a new idea and before the idea can mature, a new school board is pulling it up by the roots to examine it.

Neither instability nor stability alone determines a good working relationship between a board and a superintendent. But all things being equal, stability can be an asset. In this case, it could be a liability. The power is so centralized in one individual, that his continued service makes it difficult for change to occur.

6. *Do some school districts require employees to live within the school district? Beyond legal questions, do you believe a residency requirement is a good policy?* Some school districts have policies requiring employees either to be residents or to move into the school system within a specified period of time after employment. Ironically, the two most likely settings for such policies have been the large urban districts and the very small rural districts. Suburban districts are the least likely to be concerned with the locations of employee residences.

Proponents of such policies argue that school employees should be part of the community that pays their salaries. The one thing large urban districts and small rural districts frequently have in common is the loss of population. Thus, residence requirements are used to stem the tide of population decreases. Students should be encouraged to relate their response regarding the wisdom of such policies to a specific environment. That is, the question of residence requirements ought to be discussed within the context of a specific community. Further, the legal dimensions of residence policies could be discussed.

7. *What inferences can be drawn from the behavior of the school board president in this case?* There is a distinct possibility that what

80

occurs in this case is indicative of the board president's behavior in general. That is, the board president may be accustomed to making key decisions, telling the superintendent what to do, involving himself in the day-to-day administration of the schools, and so forth. It is also possible that the board president, even though he has been a school board member for many years, simply does not understand his proper role. Some students may speculate that the board president is motivated by personal issues such as trying to keep citizens happy so they will use his bank.

8. *What reactions could be expected if the superintendent decides to talk to each board member individually about this problem?* Although not explicitly stated, it is likely that the board president has influence over a majority (if not all) of the board members. If this is true, the superintendent's attempts to meet with each of the school board members individually is apt to result in more difficulties. The risk involved with this approach does not appear warranted given the potential outcomes.

9. *Is this case important enough for the superintendent to make a major issue out of it?* This question is difficult to answer. Many experts contend that superintendents must pick their battles carefully. A certain amount of energy (and influence and power) is typically exerted in conflict situations. If the superintendent decides to follow his own instincts on this matter and ignore the directives from his board president, he may be risking his job. Strong personalities, such as the one described in the board president, often react sternly and swiftly when their authority is challenged. Given the potentiality of legal concerns, this may be an issue that the superintendent must pursue.

OTHER SUGGESTED ACTIVITIES

1. Have your students trace the legal history of "residence clauses" in employment contracts and/or board policy.

2. Discuss the types of education and training a superintendent should have to deal with problems such as those described in this case.

81

3. Discuss the reasons why school board members often involve themselves in administrative activities.

4. Are state associations, that is, state school board associations, successful in regulating the conduct of local school boards and school board members?

SUGGESTED READINGS:

Abbott, M., & Francisco, C. (1988). Power, authority, and bureaucracy. (Ed.), *Handbook of research on educational administration,* pp.239-258. White Plains, NY: Longman.*

Black, J., & English, F. (1986). *What they don't tell you in schools of education about school administration,* pp. 46-49. Lancaster, PA: Technomic.

Castetter, W. (1985). *The personnel function in educational administration* (4th ed.), chap. 9. New York: Macmillan.

Castetter, W. (1985/86). The personnel function: Coming of age. *National Forum of Educational Administration and Supervision,* 2(3), 18-24.

Darling, J., & Ishler, R. (1989/90). Strategic conflict management: A problem-oriented approach. *National Forum of Educational Administration and Supervision Journal,* 7(1), 87-103.

Good, F. (1987). *The role of the small school district superintendent as perceived by school board presidents, superintendents, and principals in selected California school districts.* Unpublished Ed.D. thesis, University of Southern California.

Guthrie, J., & Reed, R. (1986). *Educational administration and policy,* pp. 48-55. Englewood Cliffs, NJ: Prentice-Hall.

Hanson, E. (1985). *Educational administration and organizational behavior,* (2nd ed.), chap. 10. Boston: Allyn & Bacon.*

Hoy, W., & Miskel, C. (1987). *Educational administration: Theory, research, and practice* (3rd ed.), pp 108-110. New York: Random House.*

Institute for Educational Leadership (1986). *School boards: Strengthening grass roots leadership,* chap. 2. Washington, DC: Institute for Educational Leadership.

Kowalski, T. (1989). *Planning and managing school facilities,* pp. 142-144, 151-155. New York: Praeger.

Litman, J. (1987). *Perceptions of Indiana board of education members and superintendents on the separation of leadership responsibilities.* Unpublished Ed.D. thesis, Indiana University, Bloomington.

McDaniel, T. (1986). Learn these rarely written rules of effective board service. *American School Board Journal, 173*(5), 32.

McNamee, M. (1980). Tips on being an effective board president. *American School Board Journal, 167*(7), 17.

Murray, B. (1986). *The performance of Indiana school boards: A comparative study between the performance of Indiana school boards and the Indiana School Board Association guidelines as perceived by Indiana school superintendents.* Unpublished Ph.D. thesis, Indiana State University.

Sergiovanni, T., Burlingame, M., Coombs, F., & Thurston, P. (1987). *Educational governance an administration* (2nd ed.), pp. 210-216. Englewood Cliffs, NJ: Prentice-Hall.

Weber, J. (1986). *Community politics and the school superintendent.* Ed.D. thesis, Teachers College, Columbia University.

Yukl, G. (1989). *Leadership in organizations* (2nd ed.), pp. 18-21, 34-36. Englewood Cliffs, NJ: Prentice-Hall.

*readings not included in the text

CASE 11

THE CLOSED DOOR POLICY

BACKGROUND INFORMATION

Communication systems reveal a great deal about the climate of an organization. In Case 11, we find a relatively small, but wealthy, school district in a suburban area with ample resources and fewer problems than most other public school systems. Yet, central office administrators have little contact with the chief executive officer of the organization.

Several key points emerge in this case:

1. The superintendent is a person who has worked in much larger school systems prior to coming to Placid Falls.

2. The superintendent has ambitions with regard to national visibility in professional organizations.

3. The employee faced with the problem is a relatively inexperienced female who is in an administrative post that she originally thought was beyond her experience and qualifications.

This last point is especially cogent. Many analysts point out that female administrators are more prone to move to central office positions without a great deal of building level experience. Does jumping over traditional work experiences present a problem for administrators? Does it present an especially difficult situation for women?

Another interesting area to explore is the size of the school district in relation to the behaviors noted in the case. Small school districts should have the advantage of better communication. That is, because there are fewer persons in leadership positions, one would assume that contact among these individuals would be greater. This is especially true in this case where we find a wealthy district with many resources. But as the information reveals, being small and affluent does not necessarily result in good organizational communication.

84

1. *What options does Joan have in this situation? What are the advantages and disadvantages of each?* In this specific situation, students will identify several alternatives for Joan to pursue:

    a. She could take her chances with a meeting on December 21 hoping that all goes well.

    b. She could attempt to communicate with the superintendent in some form other than making an appointment with him (e.g., calling him at home in the evening, sending him a letter).

    c. She could forget about the grant proposal.

    d. She could encourage the foundation officials to try to contact her superintendent expressing their concern about the proposal being submitted.

Many students perceive that taking a chance with the December 21 meeting is the safe thing to do. Many conclude that if something occurs to prevent the item from being included on the board agenda, Dr. Myers could not be blamed. She did her best to promulgate the issue. This, however, is not a very imaginative approach. In selecting this response, students tend to focus in on what could occur to Dr. Myers instead of the potential advantages for the school system. Trying to contact the superintendent outside of his office is a risky proposition. One can only guess how the superintendent would react to such behavior. Yet, there always is the possibility that information has been filtered and Dr. Sagossi has not been apprised of the urgency of this matter (e.g., his secretary has not shared with him the importance of the time parameters). Abandoning the grant proposal is the easiest way out. Dr. Myers eradicates her problem; but in doing so, is she meeting her professional responsibilities? Asking the foundation officials to contact the superintendent is a most risky choice. For example, the foundation officials may react negatively to such a suggestion. If the foundation officials comply, how will the superintendent react when he is contacted?

    Students should be encouraged to look at this problem in an organizational perspective. That is, the situation in the case is symptomatic of poor communication. Approaches to this specific problem ought to be predicated on ways of improving communication throughout the organization. Additionally, you can discuss the differences between organizational interests and the interests of the employee faced with the problem.

2. *Based on what you learned from reading this case, assess the climate in this school system.* Students who have completed a course in organizational theory ought to be able to deal with this assignment rather well. You should engage students in a discussion relative to open and closed organizational climates. How do closed organizations deal with communication? How do these procedures differ from those in an open organization?

3. *Based on what you learned from reading this case, assess the leadership style of the superintendent .* Dr. Sagossi appears to be an individual who believes his role is to employ dynamic leaders who will operate the school system on a day-to-day basis. His role is to gain visibility for the school system and to maintain a positive public image. In this respect, he is not a "hands on" type of leader. But is this bad? Is it an uncommon leadership style for a school district of this type? You may wish to discuss the dangers of generalization with regard to leadership styles. For example, is a leadership style always negative regardless of the context in which it occurs?

4. *Describe the differences between a "line" and a "staff" position in a school district. Does the fact that Dr. Myers functions in a staff capacity have any effect on this case?* Staff administrators do not have direct supervisory authority over other professional staff. Many students believe that titles among school administrators have universal meaning. That is not the case. Holding the title of assistant superintendent does not always connote line authority in an organization. Likewise, being a director of instruction does not necessarily mean the individual does not have direct supervisory authority over principals. Some students may contend that if Dr. Myers was in a line position, she could have dealt with this problem more directly. Clues in the case--for example, the comments of the assistant superintendent for business--suggest otherwise.

5. *Given the availability of the superintendent, do you believe that he should delegate more authority to his assistant superintendents?* It is arguable that a superintendent who is gone as much as Dr. Sagossi should allow a subordinate to make critical decisions. The case seems to indicate that although the superintendent expects his

subordinates to run the district on a day-to-day basis, he still controls key decisions (e.g., deciding what appears on the school board agenda). This question can lead to a discussion of relegating versus delegating responsibilities.

6. *Is the type of leadership behavior exhibited in this case more likely in community environments such as Placid Falls? Why or why not?* Most students readily agree that this type of leadership is more probable in an environment like Placid Falls. Some, however, will struggle to explain why this is so. In affluent communities, school boards may be more prone to accepting management styles similar to those in the private sector. In these settings, school board members may be less alarmed if the superintendent delegates a great deal of responsibility.

7. *Would you like to work in Placid Falls? Why or why not?* Students should be expected to outline the reasons for their answer. In particular, try to identify personal experiences, values, and beliefs leading students to conclusions on this question. Some students will respond with uncertainty. For these students, ask why they cannot make up their minds if they would work in this district. What additional information would they need to make up their minds?

8. *Are Joan's background and assignments typical or atypical for women who occupy central office positions?* With regard to background, there is a prevailing judgment that women are more likely to skip traditional steps (e.g., being a principal) before moving into the central office. Data supporting this observation are conclusive. Additionally, geography and other considerations often play a critical role in career patterns. With regard to assignment, the evidence is more compelling that women are more likely to find themselves in curriculum and instruction areas in central office positions. Many of these posts are designed to be staff positions. Career patterns for administrators, both male and female, are changing. It may become less likely for all administrators to follow a prescribed career path in the future.

9. *Do you think Joan is being treated differently by the superintendent because she is a woman?* There is no direct evidence in the case to support this conclusion. Some students may suggest that the superintendent's secretary treats Dr. Myers differently than

87

she would male administrators. From the information provided, it appears that most administrative staff have some difficulty in seeing the superintendent.

SUGGESTED READINGS:

Abrams, J. (1987). How superintendents can work better with others. *Education Digest*, 52(10), 26-28.

Bass, B., & Valenzi, E. (1974). Contingent aspects of effective management styles. In J. Hunt & L. Larson (Eds.), *Contingency approaches to leadership,* pp. 130-152. Carbondale, IL: Southern Illinois University Press.

Bright, K. (1987). *Leadership behaviors of Ohio school superintendents: An examination of district situational demands and perceptions by superintendents, board members, and principals.* Unpublished Ph.D.thesis, Bowling Green State University.

DeRoche, E. (1985). *How administrators solve problems,* chap. 3. Englewood Cliffs, NJ: Prentice-Hall.

Duignan, P. (1980). Administration behavior of school superintendents: A descriptive study. *Journal of Educational Administration*, 18(1), 5-26.

Garland, P., & O'Reily, R. (1976). The effect of leader-member interaction in organizational effectiveness. *Educational Administration Quarterly*, 12(3), 9-30.

Geisert, G. (1988). Participatory management: Penacex or hoax? *Educational Leadership,* 46(3), 56-59.*

Gouldner, A. (1970). About the functions of bureaucratic rules. In W. Scott (Ed.), *Social processes and social structures,* pp. 320-328. New York: Holt, Rinehart & Winston.

Hanson, E. (1985). *Educational administration and organizational behavior* (2nd ed.), chap. 9. Boston: Allyn & Bacon.

Hoy, W., & Miskel, C. (1987). *Educational administration: Theory, research, and practice* (3rd ed.), chap. 11. New York: Random House.

Hoy, W., Newland, W., & Blazovsky, R. (1977). Subordinate loyalty, esprit, and aspects of bureaucratic structure. *Educational Administration Quarterly*, 13(1), 71-85.

Immegart, G. (1988). Leadership and leader behavior. In N. Boyan (Ed.), *Handbook of research on educational administration,* pp. 259-278. White Plains, NY: Longman.

Lieberman, A. (1988). Teachers and principals: Turf, tension, and new tasks. *Phi Delta Kappan,* 70(9), 648-653.*

Loose, W., & McManus, J. (1987). Corporate management techniques in the superintendent's office. *Thrust,* 16(7), 11-13.

Meadows, B. (1990). The rewards and risks of shared leadership. *Phi Delta Kappan,* 71(7), 545-548.*

McClure, R. (1988). The evolution of shared leadership. *Educational Leadership,* 46(3), 60-62.*

Nybertg, D. (1990). Power, empowerment, and educational authority. In S. Jacobson & J. Conway (Eds.), *Educational Leadership in an age of reform.,* pp. 47-64. New York: Longman.*

O'Reilly, C., & Pondy, L. (1979). Organizational communication. In S. Kerr (Ed.), *Organizational behavior,* pp. 119-150. Columbus, Ohio Grid.

Pajak, E. (1989). *The central office supervisor of curriculum and instruction,* chap. 10. Boston: Allyn & Bacon.

St. John, J. (1985). *Superintendents' leadership style and communication satisfaction.* Unpublished Ed.D. thesis, Northern Illinois University.

Vroom, V., & Jago, A. (1988). *The new leadership: Managing participation in organizations,* chap. 7. Englewood Cliffs, NJ: Prentice-Hall

*readings not included in the text

CASE 12

CAPTAIN PUNISHMENT

BACKGROUND INFORMATION

Corporal punishment is one of the issues that tends to divide educators and communities. In recent years, the controversy has resurfaced in areas having large numbers of underprivileged children. Two factors seem quite important in this regard: (1) low socioeconomic families may not reject corporal punishment as a useful technique as readily as middle- and upper-income families, and (2) corporal punishment may be tolerated to a higher degree in schools or communities where there are numerous discipline problems.

The superintendent in this case is being placed in a position where he is being pressured to take a public position on corporal punishment. The information tells us that the school district permits such disciplinary action but case study does not clearly reveal the superintendent's personal position on this matter. Given the strong feelings in both directions, students tend to react to this case by judging that the superintendent is being placed in an impossible position. But is it a predicament for which he must assume at least part of the blame? Should policies be reviewed and/or altered only when they create public controversy?

KEY ISSUES/QUESTIONS

1. *Do you think the parents are correct in linking the discipline practices of the principal with the successes of the school?* Regardless of whether the judgment of the parents is right or wrong, it is understandable. Neither the school district nor the school's administration seems to have taken any action to dispel the perception that corporal punishment contributes to academic outcomes. Educators will readily recognize that there are a host of factors that could be contributing to positive educational outcomes at Rogers Middle School; the average citizen is less apt to draw this conclusion. Research on corporal punishment offers virtually no evidence that

90

this practice produces better learning. Many psychologists argue that it generates an opposite outcome for many students. For instance, corporal punishment may affect self-image which ultimately affects classroom performance.

2. *What are your impressions of Mr. Sanchez? Would you like to be a teacher in his building?* Most students respond to this question negatively. For some, the discipline practices will be contrary to their personal values and beliefs. Interestingly, other students see the principal as a person who is only interested in publicity and his own career. Students who support the principal's behavior may be reluctant to reveal this fact in class.

3. *Do you see any relationship between the principal's personal life and his philosophy toward discipline?* One's attitudes and practices in the area of student discipline largely are shaped by personal experience and acquired knowledge. The less the exposure to professional knowledge, the more likely one is to rely on personal experience. Psychologists note, for example, that a high percentage of children who are abused by their parents are much more likely to abuse their own children. It is possible that the principal's views toward discipline were shaped in his own childhood--a childhood marked by poverty and the absence of a father. If the principal was not exposed to information about corporal punishment in his professional education or if he rejected that information, it is probable that personal experiences are the dominant factor in his behavior.

4. *What are your impressions of the teacher who wrote the letter to the newspaper? Could he have addressed the problem in some other way?* The case tells us that the teacher attempted to discuss the issue with the principal and his immediate supervisor. The information also indicates ambivalence on the part of the superintendent. Given these circumstances, many students see the teacher's action as reasonable. Other suggested avenues for dealing with this problem include: (1) following the chain of command by making an appointment with the superintendent; (2) writing individual letters to the superintendent and school board members instead of to the newspaper; (3) reporting the matter to a child welfare agency in hopes that the agency would intervene; (4) trying

to convince the teacher association to take a stance on corporal punishment.

5. *What are your impressions of the assistant superintendent, Dr. Mackee? Did she adequately address her responsibilities in this incident?* The assistant superintendent responded to the problem much in the way that many Rogers Middle School parents responded-- equating success with corporal punishment. A higher standard should be applied to someone with a doctorate and holding a responsible position in a school system. Furthermore, the unwillingness of the assistant superintendent to act on the matter, at least to investigate it, led to the teacher's frustration. Often inaction on the part of key administrators leads to increased levels of conflict.

6. *What does the literature say about the effectiveness of corporal punishment?* As noted earlier, the vast majority of contemporary literature, both in education and psychology, takes a negative position on corporal punishment. Have your students examine articles and research studies on this topic. The recent concerns expressed toward at-risk children has spawned a number of articles focusing on student discipline, drop-out rates, and so forth.

7. *How does corporal punishment fit with the goals of middle grades education?* Among the stated goals of middle grades education is the student transition from dependence to independence. That is, students are expected to gradually take greater responsibility for their own actions during the middle grades. In this respect, corporal punishment is incongruent with developmental goals. Other goals of the middle grades include social skills, self-image, and learning to respect other individuals. Arguments against corporal punishment could be made in each of these categories.

8. *If the superintendent decides to examine policy in the area of corporal punishment, how might he go about it?* Given the controversial nature of this issue, it may be best for the superintendent to create a blue ribbon committee consisting of professionals, parents, and students. This committee should include employees as well as other citizens. The concerns of the committee's work would be the broad topic of corporal punishment and whether it should be permitted in the schools. Focusing solely on the situation at Rogers Middle School may cloud the issue and permit

emotions, rather than facts, to determine committee recommendations.

9. *What are the advantages and disadvantages of recommending a transfer for Aaron Carson?* By transferring the teacher, the superintendent would be showing support for his principal. The action, however, is very likely to be viewed as punishment by those who support Mr. Carson. Nothing in the case indicates that there are other possible reasons for such a transfer. Mr. Carson may have cause (either through law or through existing policies and union contracts) to sue the school district if he is involuntarily transferred. A transfer would be viewed as punitive if it were done prior to examining the question of corporal punishment or done in lieu of dealing with the policy elements of the conflict.

10. *In this case, committees are used by the principal to involve parents in the educational process. Under such circumstances, shouldn't the recommendations of these parents play a pivotal role in determining whether the principal is allowed to administer corporal punishment?* Parental committees can provide insight and direction. Politically, recommendations of such committees are important. These outputs must be balanced against professional knowledge, laws, policies, and the like. You can discuss the advantages and disadvantages of using committees to resolve conflict.

11. *Consider the support for the principal in the context of the social and economic dimensions of the neighborhoods served by Rogers Middle School.* As noted earlier, experience plays a critical role in shaping values and beliefs about discipline. Given a condition where many children are reared in one-parent families, corporal punishment by the school may be tolerated. Especially in homes where there is an absence of a father, the mother may be willing to have the principal become a surrogate parent. Often parents of troubled children are hopeful that the school will become a disciplinary force.

OTHER SUGGESTED ACTIVITIES

1. Invite a psychologist to discuss corporal punishment with your class.

2. See if you can obtain school board policies addressing corporal punishment.

3. Assign your students the task of determining local school policies with regard to corporal punishment.

SUGGESTED READINGS:

Andrews, R., & Soder, R. (1987). Principal leadership and student achievement. *Educational Leadership*, 44(6), 9-11.

Auer, M., & Nisenholz, B. (1987). Humanistic processes and bureaucratic structures--Are they compatible? *NASSP Bulletin*, 71(495), 96-101.

Barth, R. (1990). A personal vision of a good school. *Phi Delta Kappan*, 71(6), 424-435.*

Carey, M. (1986). School discipline: Better to be loved or feared? *Momentum*, 17(2), 20-21.

Cuban, L. (1989). The 'at-risk' label and the problem of urban school reform. *Phi Delta Kappan*, 70(10), 780-784.*

deJung, J., & Duckworth, K. (1985). *An examination of student discipline policy in three middle schools: Final report.* ERIC, Document Number ED256018.

Eberts, R., & Stone, J. (1988). Student achievement in public schools: Do principals make a difference? *Economics of Education Review*, 7(3), 291-299.

Erickson, H. (1988). The boy who couldn't be disciplined. *Principal*, 67(5), 36-37.

Glaser, W. (1990). The quality school. *Phi Delta Kappan*, 71(6), 424-435.*

Glassman, N. (1986). Student achievement and the school principal. *Education Evaluation and Policy Analysis*, 7(2), 283-296.

Helms, M. (1985). *Bureaucracy and social interaction: A study in the perceived interaction between a superintendent and campus principals.* Unpublished Ph.D. thesis, University of North Texas.

Kritsonis, W., & Adams, S. (1985/86). School discipline: Could I be part of the problem? *National Forum of Educational Administration and Supervision*, 2(2), 68-72.

Lowe, R., & Gervais, R. (1984). Tackling a problem school. *Principal*, 63(5), 8-12.

Maurer, A. (1981). *Paddles away: A psychological study of physical punishment in schools.* Palo Alto, CA: R & E Research Associates.

McCarther, E. (1985/86). Working with minority parents. *National Forum of Educational Administration and Supervision, 2*(2), 50-54.*

McDaniel, T. (1986). School discipline in perspective. *Clearing House, 59*(8), 369-370.

Nolte, M. (1985). Before you take a paddling in court, read this corporal punishment advice. *American School Board Journal, 173*(7), 27, 35.

Paquet, R. (1982). *Judicial rulings, state statutes, and state administrative regulations dealing with the use of corporal punishment in public schools.* Palo Alto, CA: R & E Research Associates.

Petty, R. (1989). Managing disruptive students. *Educational Leadership, 46*(6), 26-28.*

Reavis, C. (1986). How a lighthouse principal revitalized his school. *NASSP Bulletin, 70*(492), 44-49.

Rose, T. (1984). Current uses of corporal punishment in American public schools. *Journal of Educational Psychology, 76*(3), 427-441.

Slavin, R., & Madden, N. (1989). What works for students at-risk: A research synthesis. *Educational Leadership, 46*(5), 4-13.

Webster, L., et al. (1988). Attitudes of rural administrators toward corporal punishment. *Journal of Rural and Small Schools, 3*(1), 19-22.

Zirkel, P., & Gluckman, I. (1988). A legal brief: Constitutionalizing corporal punishment. *NASSP Bulletin, 72*(506), 105-109.

*readings not included in the text

CASE 13

THE STEPPING STONE

BACKGROUND INFORMATION

Young administrators often identify with one or more individuals who are perceived as highly successful practitioners. In this case, an inexperienced superintendent in a rural community attempts to emulate his idol, who is a superintendent in a large city school system. The young administrator fails to recognize the organizational and environmental differences between urban and rural school districts. This oversight is a critical factor in this case.

This case provides an opportunity for your students to exhibit flexibility and adaptability. You may wish to focus on the ability of students to assess problems and their willingness to engage in corrective actions. Some students will defend the superintendent's behavior; others will be critical of his actions. Have students analyze: (1) why differences occur evaluating the superintendent's behavior, and (2) the factors that lead students to make a judgment about his behavior.

KEY ISSUES/QUESTIONS

1. *To what extent do you think that Rob's attitude about going to Hallville affects his behavior in this case?* Remember that Rob only intends to stay in Hallville for two to three years. With this state of mind, he is already looking ahead to his next job. Young administrators can be so consumed with their long-term career goals that they pay inadequate attention to current challenges. This condition seems to exist here. Rather than concentrating on being highly successful in his current assignment, the superintendent sees Hallville as a routine step in his career. You may want to discuss the ramifications for Rob if he fails in this first superintendency.

2. *Was the board correct in assuming, because Rob grew up in a small town similar to Hallville, that he would be able to effectively work there?* Based on the information in the case, one could

96

conclude that the board was probably in error. It appears that the greatest influence on Rob is his former superintendent and not his childhood community. Given that Rob's idol works in a much larger community, his point of reference for practitioner success is questionable. A number of factors play a part in leadership behavior. Boyhood values and beliefs are but one ingredient. The board should have looked at the broader picture with regard to Rob's life. Furthermore, the board could have asked probing questions regarding Rob's view of administration and organizational leadership during the interview phase.

3. *To what extent is the behavior of the principals described in this study typical or atypical for small town/rural school districts?* In this day and age, generalizations about school systems are precarious. It is probable that the climate in many rural schools is somewhat informal. And although a number of rural principals may behave similarly to those described in this case, it is not fair to assume that all practitioners in rural schools share the same philosophy and leadership style as those described in this case.

4. *Is it common for young administrators to try to emulate the behavior of someone they admire?* Studies often indicate that young professionals seek significant others as models for their own behavior. These models exercise referrant power over the novices. This phenomenon is described in the literature focusing on the socialization of educators in organizations. In some instances, expert power also plays a part in the selection of role models. That is, young administrators may be influenced by leaders who are viewed as highly intelligent or skilled practitioners.

5. *Discuss the various types of power. What type of power did Dr. Smythe have over Rob?* Getting others to do what you want them to do is considered a product of power. Administrators exercise power in several ways. First, they can use legitimate power--power claimed by virtue of position within the organization. Second, they can use threats--they get individuals to do things by noting what negative things will occur if the desired behaviors are not exhibited. Third, the administrator can use the promise of reward--that is, you get the individual to act by promising them something they want if they comply. Fourth, some leaders exercise power because they are experts. Others follow their lead because the

97

leader is viewed as being an expert in a given area. Finally, the most dynamic form of influence is referrant power. Here, factors such as charisma play a critical role.

6. *What are the advantages and disadvantages of the following*
   a. the superintendent resigning immediately
   b. the superintendent apologizing to the board and agreeing that he will work to change his behavior and attitudes? Given that Rob has only been in the community a brief period of time, a resignation would be difficult to explain to prospective employers in the future. Given his age and other circumstances, resignation is not the best alternative. By staying and trying to work things out, Rob will be exhibiting maturity and he also will permit himself to learn from his experiences. It may not be necessary to formally apologize to mend the fences, but it is important to create better communication linkages in the school system. Rob needs to spend some time looking at issues from the perspective of his employees. He needs to understand the values and beliefs of the Hallville residents. Young administrators may believe that organizations must change to accommodate them.

7. *Is the superintendent's assessment that informality breeds inefficiency accurate? Why or why not?* This assessment is grounded in classical theory. According to this theory, social distance from employees permits the superintendent to remain objective in his dealings with subordinates. There are leaders who are capable of establishing trusting relationships with employees without compromising responsibility. You may wish to have your students describe superintendents they know and to assess their behaviors with regard to socializing with employees.

8. *Do you think the school board knows that Rob is only planning to stay in Hallville for three years? What leads you to your conclusion?* It is difficult to determine the answer to this question. On the one hand, Rob does rent, rather than buy, a house. Some will see this as a sign that he does not plan to stay. On the other hand, many young administrators cannot afford to buy a house. Hallville residents apparently like the community and they may assume that Rob shares this sentiment. The case simply does not supply sufficient information for us to determine what the board knows about Rob's career plans.

9. *What alternatives could Rob have pursued to implement change in the school district?* One possibility would have been for Rob to attempt to engage his employees in conversations about the behaviors he disliked. By doing so, he could have learned their viewpoints. Additionally, Rob could have shared his concerns and explained why the behaviors bothered him so much. Discussion could have led to mutually agreeable solutions. To simply mandate change, via directives, was not a good choice of action under the circumstances.

10. *Did Rob do the right thing by trying to emulate the successful practices of an outstanding superintendent?* There certainly is nothing wrong with having a role model. What created the problem for Rob was his inability to inject organizational and environmental differences when trying to imitate his idol. He did not understand or adequately weigh the importance of these two variables in determining whether given leadership behaviors would be successful and/or accepted. Further, he fails to recognize that individual traits play some part in one's ability to use certain practices. For instance, an extroverted personality may permit one to work more effectively with groups.

OTHER SUGGESTED ACTIVITIES

1. Invite a specialist in job placement to your class to comment on this case.

2. Have your students identify factors that are substantially different in the climates of large and small school systems.

3. Discuss the merits and potential pitfalls of long-range career planning.

4. Should a school board employ a superintendent who admits that he or she would only stay three years? Have your students debate this question.

SUGGESTED READINGS:

Alvey, D., & Underwood, K. (1985). When boards and superintendents clash, it's over the balance of school power. *American School Board Journal*, 172(10), 21-25.

Black, J., & English, F. (1986). *What they don't tell you in schools of education about school administration,* pp. 293-307. Lancaster, PA: Technomic.

Boynton, M. (1985). *Practical P. R. techniques for small schools.* ERIC, Document Number ED270281.

Burnham, J. (1989). Superintendents on the fast track. *The School Administrator*, 46(9), 18-19.*

Campion, M., & Lord, R. (1982). A control systems conceptualization of the goal-setting and changing process. *Organizational Behavior and Human Performance*, 30, 265-287.

Clark, D., & Astuto, T. (1988). Paradoxical choice options in organizations. In D. Griffiths, R. Stout, & P. Forsyth, (Eds.), *Leaders for America's schools,* (pp. 112-130). Berkeley, CA: McCutchan.

Guthrie, J., & Reed, R. (1986). *Educational administration and policy,* pp. 166-175. Englewood Cliffs, NJ: Prentice-Hall.

Fuqua, A. (1983). *Professional attractiveness, inside sponsorship, and perceived paternalism as predictors of upward mobility of public school superintendents.* Unpublished Ph.D. thesis, Virginia Polytechnic Institute and State University.

Hopkins, R. (1989). How to survive and succeed as the chief school executive. *The School Administrator*, 46(9), 15-17.*

Immegart, G. (1988). Leadership and leader behavior. In N. Boyan (Ed.), *Handbook of research on educational administration,* pp. 259-277. White Plains, NY: Longman.

Jacobson, S. (1988). Effective superintendents of small, rural districts. *Journal of Rural and Small Schools*, 2(2), 17-21.

Kanchler, C., & Unruh, W. (1987). Frequency and direction of managerial occupational change. *Career Development Quarterly*, 35(4), 305-315.*

Oberg, T. (1986). The ecstasy and the agony: Administrative success on one level does not guarantee success on another. *Journal of Educational Public Relations*, 9(2), 28-31.

Schaal, B. (1987). *Perceived conflict among Wisconsin superintendents and its relationship to selected factors.* Unpublished Ph.D. thesis, University of Nebraska, Lincoln.

Sergiovanni, T., Burlingame, M., Coombs, F., & Thurston, P. (1987). *Educational governance and administration* (2nd ed.), pp. 206-219; 384-416. Englewood Cliffs, NJ: Prentice-Hall.

St. John, J. (1985). *Superintendents' leadership style and communication satisfaction.* Unpublished Ed.D. thesis, Northern Illinois University.

Toy, S. (1985). Use this ten point plan to bolster community rapport. *Executive Educator, 7*(6), 23-25.

Yukl, G. (1989). *Leadership in organizations* (2nd ed.), chap. 8. Englewood Cliffs, NJ: Prentice-Hall.

* readings not included in the text

CASE 14

SUCCESS IS SPELLED "PR, PR, PR"

<u>BACKGROUND INFORMATION</u>

Role perceptions of leadership may vary significantly within school districts. For example, teachers and school board members may differ substantially in their expectations of the superintendent. In this case, a superintendent decides to devote a large amount of his time to working in the area of public relations. He delegates most managerial tasks to a deputy. Gradually, the deputy becomes disenchanted with the arrangement, concluding that she is doing all the work and the superintendent is getting all the praise.

Students typically have mixed reactions when assuming the role of superintendent. Consider some of the possible courses of action:

1. The superintendent agrees to change his ways and to devote more time to the day-to-day operations in the district.

2. The superintendent agrees to give his deputy a substantial increase in salary in an attempt to prevent her from leaving, but her role remains unchanged.

3. The superintendent engages in discussions with his staff. He does so in an attempt to better understand their concerns and to try to explain his administrative style.

4. The superintendent concludes that he made a mistake in naming this person to be his deputy and removes her from the position.

5. The superintendent requests the school board to formally communicate to the staff their expectation that the superintendent devote much of his energy to public relations.

One interesting dynamic of this case is the fact that the superintendent is a male and the deputy superintendent is a female. That spawns the question, would the superintendent behave in the same fashion if his deputy was a man? Or would the deputy behave the same way if the superintendent was a female?

KEY ISSUES/QUESTIONS

1. *Do you believe that Dr. Howard is being fair with the superintendent?* Some students will empathize with the deputy superintendent. They will see her as a hard working individual who is not receiving due credit for her work. On the other hand, the superintendent is doing primarily what he was hired to do. Should an organization permit subordinates to question the role that is played by the chief executive officer? What would happen if Dr. Marini decided to abandon his public relations efforts and become more concerned with day-to-day administrative operations? These are critical queries that should be raised with your students as they review this case. One critical question that hopefully will be asked by one of your students relates to whether the deputy was aware of the school board's expectations for Dr. Marini.

2. *Is it common for administrative staff members to believe that their work is not properly recognized or compensated?* Indeed, many employees in all types of organizations perceive that their work does not receive proper acclaim. This factor is often overlooked by principals and superintendents who fail to give periodic kudos to those doing outstanding work. Literature in school administration contains many references to task-oriented versus person-oriented leaders. Students should be encouraged to review this literature and to identify ways that the superintendent could have provided recognition to his deputy.

3. *Is Dr. Marini, in your opinion, doing a good job as superintendent? Why or why not?* If this question is viewed from a microperspective, that is, with regard solely to what the board of education desires, the answer is probably yes. If the question is addressed in the wider organizational perspective, the answer is less clear. It is likely that the superintendent is not sensitive to the feelings of his high ranking staff members. Additionally, he does not appear to be well informed regarding what is actually occurring in the school system. Given these circumstances, some students will

criticize the superintendent's behavior. Is it sufficient for the superintendent to please the school board?

4. *What are the advantages and disadvantages of Dr. Marini deciding to reassign his deputy superintendent?* One advantage would be to eradicate the problem, at least temporarily. Additionally, some students may view this action as indicative of a forceful leader. On the down side, the deputy is doing a very good job. The superintendent has to ask himself if he can find someone else who can do as well. Immediately jumping to the conclusion that the deputy should be replaced may indicate impulsive behavior. The real challenge is to identify options that keep the deputy in the job and permit the superintendent to continue his public relations efforts. You can suggest that changes in both of their leadership behaviors may be needed.

5. *Given the information in this case, do you believe that Dr. Marini is in a position to meet the demands of his deputy?* The information in the case makes it appear that the deputy is solely interested in money. But is this really true? How much of her dissatisfaction relates to ego? How much relates to a bitterness that she is not receiving due credit for her work? If the matter were simply one of dollars, it is likely that giving her a substantial raise would resolve the problem. The superintendent should diagnose the situation before deciding to pursue any given solution. Simply giving a large raise may not eradicate the problem. Thus, Dr. Marini probably could meet the salary demands of his deputy, but he may conclude that this is not the best solution.

6. *What are the advantages and disadvantages of the superintendent deciding to spend more time working directly with the day-to-day operations of the school district?* By knowing more about the school system, its strengths, weaknesses, and needs, the superintendent may be in a better position to deal with public relations. Additionally, he may come closer to fulfilling the role expectations of his senior staff. However, if he changes his behavior, he may suffer a decline in public relations--an area very important to the school board. Some students may note that quickly changing behaviors sends the wrong signals to the administrative staff and school board. That is, the superintendent may be perceived as an individual who alters priorities when under criticism.

7. *In school districts of twenty to thirty thousand students, is it common for the superintendent to spend time in the school buildings? What basis do you have for your response?* The majority of students conclude that superintendents in large school districts spend less time in school buildings than superintendents in small school districts. Increasingly, superintendents are exhibiting a range of individual leadership styles. Size of school district does not necessarily dictate how superintendents spend their time. Some superintendents in very small districts, for example, may never visit schools. By contrast, there are superintendents in large districts who devote 50 to 70 percent of their time to visiting schools and talking to principals, teachers, and students. Again, generalizations are prone to error.

8. *What information is not presented in this case that you think would be important to formulating a response?* Students will identify a number of factors, but among the most common are: (1) knowing whether the senior staff of associates and the deputy were aware of the role expectations that the school board had of the superintendent; (2) knowing whether the deputy's assessment that the superintendent did not know what was going on in the school district was accurate; (3) knowing whether Dr. Marini had the resources to give his deputy a large salary increase; (4) knowing for sure that the deputy's comments reflected the feelings of other senior staff administrators.

9. *What could Dr. Marini have done to avoid this confrontation with his deputy?* The case does not provide evidence of discussions that were held between the superintendent and the deputy prior to her acceptance of the position. It is possible, and even likely, that Dr. Marini did not do a good job of detailing how he would spend his time. In addition, it appears that the top two administrators were not communicating regularly about job responsibilities. The case seems to suggest that the concerns of the deputy were not discussed until she became extremely frustrated. On the other hand, the deputy's frustration may be linked to the superintendent's tendency to take credit for all accomplishments.

10. *What could Dr. Howard have done to avoid the confrontation?* The responsibility for open communication is shared by the superintendent and the deputy. Dr. Howard should have raised

questions and concerns prior to the point of declaring an ultimatum. A good relationship between a superintendent and his staff depends on a willingness to have candid discussions. Apparently this did not occur. Given the level of responsibility relegated to the deputy, it seems reasonable to expect that the two top leaders would have spent more time communicating with each other.

OTHER SUGGESTED ACTIVITIES

1. Invite someone from your university who specializes in organizational communication to visit your class to discuss the dynamics of this case.

2. Engage your students in a discussion relative to the effects of salary on keeping employees happy.

3. Have your students develop a list of positive outcomes that could be derived from this conflict situation if it is properly managed.

SUGGESTED READINGS:

Bagin, R. (1984). *Evaluating your school PR investment.* ERIC, Document Number ED264650.

Black, J., & English, F. (1986). *What they don't tell you in schools of education about school administration,* chap. 12. Lancaster, PA: Technomic.

Boyd, W. (Ed.). (1979). *Education and Urban Society,* 11, 275-431 (special theme issue: Declining school enrollments: Politics and management).

Chand, K. (1984). *Superintendent-community relationships in the United States and Alaska.* ERIC, Document Number ED249616.

Danzberger, J., & Usdan, M. (1984). Building partnerships: The Atlanta experience. *Phi Delta Kappan,* 6(6), 393-396.

Foster, W. (1986). *Paradigms and Promises,* chap. 8. Buffalo, NY: Prometheus Books.

Goldhammer, K. (1983). Evolution in the profession. *Educational Administration Quarterly,* 19(3), 249-272.

Heller, R., & Pautler, A. (1990). The administrator of the future Combining instructional and managerial leadership. In S. Jacobson & J. Conway (Eds.), *Educational leadership in an age of reform*, pp. 131-143. New York: Longman.*

Hess, F. (1983). Evolution in practice. *Educational Administration Quarterly*, 19(3), 223-248.

Hopkins, R. (1989). How to survive and succeed as a chief school executive. *The School Administrator*, 46(9), 15-17.*

Hoy, W., & Miskel, C. (1987). *Educational administration: Theory, research, practice* (3rd ed.), pp. 302-309. New York: Random House.

Lindsay, C. (1986). Try these tonics to pep up schools. *Executive Educator*, 8(4), 28, 38.

Love, R. (1982). *Mayors and superintendents: What techniques might be used to improve partnerships.* ERIC, Document Number ED226440.

March, J. (1984). How we talk and how we act: Administrative theory and administrative life. In T. Sergiovanni & J. Corbally (Eds.), *Leadership and organizational culture*, pp. 18-35. Urbana, IL: University of Illinois Press.*

McLaughlin, M. (1987). Forge alliances with key groups. *Executive Educator*, 9(11), 21, 30.

Newell, C. (1978). *Human behavior in educational administration*, chap. 10. Englewood Cliffs, NJ: Prentice-Hall.

Pajak, E. (1989). *The central office supervisor of curriculum and instruction*, chap. 4. Boston: Allyn & Bacon.

Sergiovanni, T., Burlingame, M., Coombs, F., & Thurston, P. (1987). *Educational governance and administration* (2nd ed.), chap. 7. Englewood Cliffs, NJ: Prentice-Hall.

Shakeshaft, C. (1989). *Women in educational administration* (updated ed.), chap. 6. Newbury Park, CA: Sage Publications.

Stout, S., et al. (1987). Career transitions of supervisors and subordinates. *Journal of Vocational Behavior*, 30(2), 124-137.

Worner, R. (1989). Thirteen ways to help your inherited staff keep you afloat. *Executive Educator*, 11(5), 19-21.

Yukl, G. (1989). *Leadership in organizations* (2nd ed.), pp. 153-157. Englewood Cliffs, NJ: Prentice-Hall.

*readings not included in text

CASE 15

SORCERER WILL HELP YOU SPELL IT

BACKGROUND INFORMATION

In recent years, censorship has resurfaced as a concern for public education. Ranging from statewide efforts to regulate textbooks to parental pressures at the local school level, administrators increasingly have had to respond to questions about instructional materials used in the schools. Case 15 entails a concerted effort by a group of parents in a suburban school district to remove a software program from the list of supplemental materials being used in an elementary school gifted and talented program.

Several key issues emerge in this case. Among the more cogent are the following: (1) To what extent should principals be held accountable for materials that are used in their buildings?; (2) How does the superintendent weigh parental input against professional staff opinions?; (3) Should supplemental materials be adopted (purchased) in a less formal manner than textbooks?; (4) If the principals had acted differently on receiving the complaints, could they have reduced the intensity of the conflict?

In responding to the challenge outlined in this case, the superintendent needs to ponder these and other questions. The situation has reached a point where it appears he must declare one party (either the parents or the teachers) to be the winner. Creative students seek to find some way allowing both parties to claim partial victory. Is there some way to bring the parties together to find a solution acceptable to all? This is a cogent question for the students as they review this case.

KEY ISSUES/QUESTIONS

1. *Evaluate the process for purchasing materials for the gifted and talented program in this school district.* If principals are to be accountable for all materials used in their schools, they should play some role in material selection and approval. The purchasing system

described in this case bypasses the principals. In all likelihood, little thought was given to potential problems when this purchasing procedure was enacted. You may wish to focus on ways of improving the procedure to assure principals input in materials acquisitions (see number 9).

2. *Whom do you believe should be held accountable for this problem?* Students tend to disagree in answering this question. Some contend that principals remain accountable even though they do not participate in the processing of the purchase order. Other students point the finger at the assistant superintendent. Interestingly, some students blame the teachers. Those that take this position argue that as professionals, the teachers should be held accountable for decisions they make, especially decisions related to instruction and instructional materials. This latter judgment may be related to the growing acceptance of the concept of teacher empowerment (see number 7).

3. *Is it sufficient to tell the parents, as Dr. Youngman suggested to the principals, that use of the materials is voluntary? Why or why not?* It is unlikely that the unhappy parents will accept this response as being satisfactory. First, the parents are probably concerned that their children will still have contact with the materials in school. Second, their objections are so strong that nothing short of removing the materials from the school is apt to suffice. Parents do not want to be put in a position where they must tell their children not to use certain materials.

4. *Is there anything about the community in which this occurs that has implications for potential solutions?* The case at least hints that this is a middle-class suburb. Demographically, such communities usually consist of individuals who are well educated. If these assumptions are accurate, it may be fruitful to try to bring the teachers and parents together. Such a contact would permit a sharing of views and an open discussion of possible solutions. If this case occurred in an area where the level of parental education was low, it would be less likely that parents would be willing to meet face-to-face with teachers to discuss the issue. They may be intimidated by educators.

5. *What is your assessment of the position taken by the three elementary principals?* Obviously, none of the principals involved wants to assume responsibility. In fact, all three clearly attempt to wash their hands of the problem. Many superintendents would be disappointed in this behavior. Effective administrative teams cooperate to seek solutions rather than engaging in the assignment of blame. It could be that the organizational climate of this school district discourages such collaboration. You may want to inject the literature on failure avoidance behavior in relation to this question.

6. *What is your assessment of Dr. Youngman's behavior in this case?* Administrators in larger organizations routinely sign hundreds of documents in a week. Does this reality absolve the assistant superintendent of responsibility in approving the material in question? Should Dr. Youngman have consulted with the principals before approving the material? These are questions students typically ask when they focus on the behavior of the assistant superintendent. Students tend to place some blame with Dr. Youngman and many are disappointed in his lack of leadership once the problem evolves. The potentiality for conflict is increased when a school district does not have formal review procedures for acquiring supplemental materials.

7. *Relate the problem in this case with the movement toward teacher empowerment.* Oftentimes, organizations adopt procedural changes without fully understanding the range of possible implications of such alterations. Teacher empowerment is designed to provide instructors greater latitude in making instructional decisions. This case raises at least one question as to how far that authority should extend. As school districts move toward school site management or other reforms that provide greater professional autonomy to teachers, a number of similar queries are inevitable. Teacher empowerment also entails responsibilities. In this regard, the teachers may be held more accountable for selecting materials than has been generally true in the past.

8. *What are the advantages and disadvantages of the superintendent deciding to support Mrs. Oberfeld and keeping the program among the supplemental materials in the gifted and talented curriculum?* In deciding to retain the materials, the superintendent is stating his faith in the judgment of the teachers. This decision would be viewed

positively by the professional staff--at least the teachers. On the other hand, the continuance of the materials may result in even more public pressure. How will this pressure affect the school board? By not removing the materials, the superintendent is, in essence, giving his personal approval. He no longer can distance himself from the decision. By contrast, removal of the material may cause serious problems with the teachers. They may view the superintendent as being vulnerable to public pressure and a leader who does not respect teacher opinions.

9. *Identify an alternative method for selecting instructional materials that may have avoided this problem.* If the school system had some form of selection/screening process, the conflict may have been less severe. This is especially true if the process included parents. It is for this very reason that many public school systems have created committees of teachers, parents, administrators, and even students to review materials that may be purchased. Additionally, no system should allow principals to be removed from the process. They should play some role in approving materials and equipment. Removing the principal from the process signals a belief that the administrators are not totally responsible for what occurs in their buildings.

10. *Do you agree with the assessment of Mrs. Oberfeld that there are fundamentalist-type parents who want to control the entire curriculum of public schools?* This issue has been raised in many communities. Examples include the teaching of sex education, the teaching of evolution, and the treatment of health-related issues (e.g., AIDS, substance abuse). One should be careful, however, to draw sweeping generalizations on this topic. Community values vary markedly from one part of the country to another. Each issue, each problem, should be studied within the context in which it occurs. Many parents are genuinely concerned about a single issue and their goal may not be to control the entire curriculum of public education.

SUGGESTED READINGS:

Bailey, G. (1988). Guidelines for improving the textbook/material selection process. *NASSP Bulletin, 72*(515), 87-92.

Bryson, J. (1983). *Conservative pressures on curriculum.* ERIC, Document Number ED232307.

Clark, E. (1986). A slow, subtle exercise in censorship. *School Library Journal,* 32(7), 93-96.*

DeRoche, E. (1985). *How administrators solve problems,* chap. 9. Englewood Cliffs, NJ: Prentice-Hall.

Donelson, K. (1987). Censorship: Heading off the attack. *Educational Horizons,* 65, 167-170.

Donelson, K. (1987). Six statements/questions from the censors. *Phi Delta Kappan,* 69, 208-214.

Georgiady, N., & Romano, L. (1987). Censorship--Back to the front burner. *Middle School Journal,* 18, 12-13.

Guthrie, J., & Reed, R. (1986). *Educational administration and policy,* pp. 333-343. Englewood Cliffs, NJ: Prentice-Hall.

McCarthy, M. (1985). Curriculum controversies and the law. *Educational Horizons,* 64(3), 53-55.

McCarthy, M. (1988). Curriculum censorship: Values in conflict. *Educational Horizons,* 67(1-2), 26-34.

Pajak, E. (1989). *The central office supervisor of curriculum and instruction,* chap. 11. Boston: Allyn & Bacon.

Parker, F. (1988). Textbook censorship and secular humanism in perspective. *Religion and Public Education,* 15(3), 253-261.*

Pierard, R. (1983). What's new about the new right. *Contemporary Education,* 54(3), 194-200.

Pierard, R. (1987). The new religious right and censorship. *Contemporary Education,* 58(3), 131-137.

Rowell, C. (1986). Allowing parents to screen textbooks would lead to anarchy in the schools. *Chronicle of Higher Education,* 33 (November 26), 34.

Sendor, B. (1988). Good cases make bad law, and this curriculum ruling suggests the opposite also can be true. *American School Board Journal,* 175(9), 7, 37.*

Snyder, K., & Anderson, R. (1986). *Managing productive schools: Toward an ecology,* pp. 333-341. Orlando, FL: Academic Press College Division.

Udow, R. (1988). You can combat censorship. *Educational Leadership,* 45(8), 14.*

Weil, J. (1988). Dealing with censorship: Policy and procedures. *Education Digest,* 53(5), 23-25.

Zirkel, P., & Gluckman, I. (1986). Objections to curricular material on religious grounds. *NASSP Bulletin*, <u>70</u>(488), 99-103.

*readings not included in the text

WHOSE PHILOSOPHY WILL CONTROL COLLECTIVE BARGAINING?

BACKGROUND INFORMATION

This case places a relatively young, female superintendent in a very challenging position. The situation offers opportunities to explore several major areas of school administration:

1. The development of values and beliefs about collective bargaining.

2. The effect of personal philosophy on administrative behavior.

3. The struggle for power among organizational groups.

4. Administrative team relationships.

5. The relationship between the administrative team and the school board.

Values and beliefs regarding collective bargaining, once formed, usually result in rigid thinking about the process. In this case, two such positions collide. The superintendent believes that direct contact with key union officials will bring results; by contrast, the personnel director is convinced the teachers' union is driven by unworthy motives.

Large school systems in urban areas frequently have: (1) a number of administrators who worked their way up through the ranks of that district, and (2) a number of administrators who formerly belonged to a teachers' union and held leadership positions in the union. Additionally, the boards in such districts often prefer to employ a superintendent from the "outside." All of these conditions are found in this case.

Large systems tend to be quite bureaucratic. The superintendent in a large urban system, for example, rarely becomes involved directly in the bargaining process. This case raises some challenging questions about organizational theory and leadership style. In a typical graduate class, students can be expected to exhibit different reactions to the superintendent's behavior. One of your goals is to get students to understand how their own values and beliefs affect their perceptions of the leadership behavior.

Regardless of which overall position students take in this case, they should be able to find support in the literature. Writers offer distinctively different views on the topic of collective bargaining. In general, material focusing on organizational theory and leadership tends to support the use of interventions to resolve conflict (e.g., see Yukl 1989 from reading list at the end of the case). By contrast, material focusing on collective bargaining tends to be pessimistic about collaboration with public sector unions (e.g., see the work of Lieberman, 1984; 1988).

THE CHALLENGE

The response of the student will be largely determined by personal perceptions regarding issues such as bureaucratic practices, collective bargaining, collaboration, leadership style, and decisive leadership behavior. In general the student is apt to give one of three responses:

1. Ignore the letter and continue to follow a pattern of trying to build trust and cooperation with the union leadership.

2. Discontinue the meetings and essentially do what the administrators are requesting.

3. Avoid making an immediate decision by requesting more information, more time, and the like.

If students avoid an immediate decision, they should be required to identify the reasons for selecting this alternative. If they want more data, for instance, then they should be prepared to identify the information they desire. Additionally, the advantages and disadvantages relative to delaying a decision should be identified and weighed. If students opt for either continuing attempts at collaboration or discontinuing meetings with the union officials, they should be asked to outline a justification for the choice.

115

KEY ISSUES/QUESTIONS

1. *Did Janice do the right thing in arranging a meeting with the union leadership?* Students may identify a whole host of defenses or criticisms regarding the superintendent's decision to meet with the teachers' union leadership in her first week on the job. Listed here are some of the more common responses you can anticipate.

Possible defenses of the superintendent's behavior include:

    a. She wanted to change the image the union had of the administration of the school district.

    b. She was taking risks because the board wanted the bargaining problem resolved.

    c. She believed that conflict required management and that was her job.

    d. She believed that working directly with people and getting them to trust you is a productive approach to difficult problems.

Possible criticisms of the superintendent's behavior include:

    a. She risks losing the loyalty of her own staff.

    b. She knew too little of the nature of the problems in the district before getting involved.

    c. She undermined the authority of the board's negotiating team.

    d. She is sending messages to the teachers' union that the board may not necessarily support the position of its own bargaining team.

Some students also may raise a question regarding timing. For example, they may be receptive to the superintendent having such a meeting, but they may feel the timing was wrong. Others may conclude that the meeting, per se, was acceptable but that the superintendent should not have met with the union officials alone.

2. *How do personal values and beliefs affect one's perspective on collective bargaining?* Basic values and beliefs about people, about leadership, and about conflict exemplify factors that affect decisions. For instance, believing that you can trust people, believing that persons will be more cooperative if you show that you care about them are fundamental to this case. It is essential to point out the differences in professional experience between the superintendent and her staff. There is no indication that Janice Melton has ever worked in a large, urban school district prior to accepting the job in

Washington City. By contrast, most of her top aides are persons who gained most or all of their administrative experience in such a system. This condition allows you to ask cogent questions regarding organizational differences, organizational effects on leadership behavior, the impact of the environmental field in large, urban districts, and so forth. Also, you may wish to have a discussion focusing on the importance of the superintendent's previous experiences vis-à-vis gender and age (factors that may be considered more important by some students when they analyze this case).

3. *List the advantages and disadvantages of Dr. Melton agreeing to do what four of her top five aides are asking?* Many administrators believe that their number one obligation is to their immediate staff. That is, the administrative team must come first. As students analyze this case, some of the possible advantages that emerge with regard to the superintendent agreeing to cease contact with the union include the following:

    a. The superintendent exhibits her support for immediate subordinates.

    b. The central office staff is apt to be more supportive (and loyal).

    c. The superintendent exhibits that she may have made a mistake and is willing to admit it.

    d. The superintendent exhibits that she is willing to listen to advice from her staff.

Some potential disadvantages include the following:

    a. She will be perceived as a weak leader.

    b. She will further antagonize the union because they may assume they have been misled.

    c. She may jeopardize her position with board members who believe the conflict should be resolved as quickly as possible.

    d. She will give the perception that she is an inexperienced leader prone to making quick and uninformed decisions.

4. *Discuss the procedures under which Dr. Melton was employed. Given what you know about the district and its problems, was this a good procedure?* The details in the case regarding the superintendent's employment are somewhat sketchy. The process may be attacked from two separate directions. First, there are certainly some legal questions that could be raised. For instance, did the board adequately advertise the position? Were all employees

given an opportunity to apply? The legal dimension allows you to infuse your own state laws as well as federal laws governing employment practices.

The employment practices used here also can be challenged on grounds of appropriateness. The following questions exemplify this dimension:

a. Did the board adequately assess its own needs before charging off to hire a new superintendent?

b. Is it appropriate to allow one individual to have so much influence over who is interviewed (as did the professor in this case)?

c. Should the board have involved other groups in the superintendent search?

d. Did the board do an adequate job of evaluating Janice Melton's qualifications?

One related exercise would be to have the students formulate an alternative process for searching for a superintendent given the circumstances of this case.

5. *Evaluate the behavior of David Zellers.* Some students may see David Zellers as a hero in this case. This is especially true for students who have a very negative attitude toward collective bargaining and unions. To these individuals, Zellers may be the one with the correct perception; and given this judgment, they may view Zellers's behavior as appropriate. Most students, however, are likely to challenge his wisdom in taking on a new superintendent in her first week on the job. This challenge may take the form of a bureaucratic argument (the subordinate has no right to challenge the boss) or a political expediency (it is stupid to jeopardize your standing with a new superintendent).

It may be beneficial to discuss the fact that Zellers's first attempt at expressing his views was done one-on-one. That is, he attempted to communicate with the new superintendent confidentially. The letter, however, draws in a wider audience even though it is marked "confidential." Students who are critical of Zellers should be asked the following questions:

a. Do you think a person in Zellers's position should ever offer advice to the superintendent about her contacts related to collective bargaining?

b. If yes, how could Zellers have done a better job of communicating?

6. *If you were Janice Melton would you share the letter with the board president (and the remainder of the board)?* The response to this query is undoubtedly affected by whether the superintendent agrees to follow the advice in the letter. If students believe that the superintendent should follow the advice, they are not likely to share the letter (after all, part of the letter suggests changing board member perceptions).

Some students will perceive the letter as an attempt at intimidation. Their reaction may be to turn to the school board for assistance and support. There is, however, a degree of risk in this option. The board may perceive such action as a weakness (i.e., Janice cannot handle her own problems). Or the board may decide to become more directly involved in collective bargaining. And finally, the board may demand more firings, thus creating additional conflict.

Students who respond that they would share the letter should be asked the following questions:

a. Would you inform all the board members or just the president?

b. What are your motives in sharing the letter with the board president?

c. How would you share the letter (i.e., would you call him, would you mail a copy to him)?

Students who respond that they would not share the letter should be asked the following questions:

a. What potential dangers are there in not sharing the letter?

b. What are your motives in not sharing the letter?

c. Would you share the letter with anyone else?

7. *Is it fair to generalize that individuals who acquired their current positions via internal promotions tend to behave in the same manner?* This question is best discussed in the context of organizational theory. Persons who have been a part of an organization for a long period of time are likely to be aware of: (1) how the organization functions, (2) values and beliefs prevalent in the organization, and (3) the existence of informal and formal groups within the organization and their degrees of power. Thus, support for the former superintendent may in large measure be related to the belief that "he was one of us." The administrative staff who moved up through the ranks of the school district are likely to constitute an informal group in the organization (distinguished from all

119

administrators who are a formal group). This group is apt to have common goals even though those goals are not formalized. Additionally, the power of such informal groups to affect individual behavior is well-documented in the literature (e.g., the well-known "Hawthorne Studies" authored by Elton Mayo). A discussion of how this group might be struggling for power against the teachers' union can be quite interesting for the students.

8. *Assess Janice's leadership style of confronting issues directly.* Historically, educational administration devoted a great deal of attention to trait theory. These inquiries were based on the notion that successful leaders possess specific traits (e.g., height, emotional stability). Students are likely to discuss the superintendent's initiative as if her reaction to this one incident was indicative of her leadership style. But is the information in the case sufficient to reach this decision? Even if it were, one can find an incongruence here with regard to traits commonly associated with success (e.g., decisiveness versus adaptability to varying situations). There is no way of knowing from the information in this case whether or not the superintendent consciously weighed environmental and organizational conditions prior to making a decision to meet with the union leadership. If she had, her motives may be quite complex. If she had not, then her behavior might be indicative of a trait she possesses.

This case presents one opportunity to discuss the weaknesses of trait theory. The work of Bass and Stogdill (see readings at end of this case) may be particularly helpful to understanding the relationship between traits and situational leadership. It also can lead to a discussion of making generalizations about leaders from limited information. Some may view the superintendent as impulsive or inflexible (she is unable to change her leadership behavior even though she is now working in a much different school district than she is accustomed to).

9. *In your opinion, was Janice Melton ready to be superintendent in such a complex school district?* Without linkage to specific criteria, the responses students will give will be purely conjecture. Often individuals develop beliefs that readiness is a quantitative measure expressed in chronological age, years of experience, or academic degrees.

The key question is whether the board was able to accurately assess the specific leadership skills and knowledge required and whether Janice Melton met all or most of these criteria. The sketchy information made available in the case suggests that the board probably did not spend a great deal of time studying the district's leadership needs.

It is essential to point out that readiness for a key administrative position cannot be measured by any single standard. A whole host of factors can be involved. Readiness is accurately judged when: (1) there is an accurate list of expectations, (2) there is accurate information regarding a candidate's strengths and weaknesses, and (3) there is congruence between expectations and capabilities.

10. *Do you think the administrators who wrote the letter have a proper perspective of collective bargaining?* Practicing administrators and professors of educational administration often disagree about the merits of collective bargaining in public education. The administrators who wrote the letter exhibit a belief that collective bargaining is a power struggle. Thus they believe that administrators, as a group, must remain united. They view the superintendent's initiatives as sending the wrong messages to the teachers' union. Furthermore, they believe that some board members and the superintendent are naive when it comes to negotiations.

You may wish to have students discuss the two opposing positions regarding interventions in the formal collective bargaining process: (1) interventions are good because they exhibit trust and understanding in the other side's positions, and (2) interventions create a perception of divisiveness among the board/administrative team.

11. *What are the possible advantages and disadvantages for Tom Zibick, the assistant superintendent who refused to sign the letter?* The case provides no information regarding the reason why this assistant superintendent refused to sign the letter that was sent to the superintendent. The possible advantages of his refusal include the following:

   a. He exhibits his loyalty to the superintendent.
   b. He exhibits his respect for the superintendent's authority.

c. He exhibits that he is an independent thinker who will not be influenced by group pressures.

The possible disadvantages include the following:

a. He angers his peers who perceive him as not adhering to the "group" standards.

b. His actions may be interpreted by some as self-serving.

c. His actions may be interpreted as an indication of indifference toward the process of collective bargaining.

You may wish to have students develop a list of possible reasons why this administrator did not sign the letter. Some possibilities are listed here:

a. He respects the superintendent's authority (or judgment) and does want to second guess.

b. He sees this as an opportunity to advance his status with the new superintendent.

c. He believes that what the superintendent is attempting is correct.

d. He fears potential repercussions if he signs the letter (either from the superintendent or the board).

e. He does not feel sufficiently informed to take a position on the matter.

f. He is sympathetic to the union and supports the superintendent's efforts.

12. *Administrators often rely on behaviors that have proven successful in past experiences. Is this a good practice?* Contingency theories provide a wealth of information useful to analyzing answers to this question. Every situation is a composite of a myriad of variables. The existing environmental field, organizational dynamics, past practices, and so forth are contributing factors. You may wish to give the students an example of an administrator who is highly successful in one school (or school system) and who fails to adjust behaviors after assuming a new position. The same behaviors that produce success in one school district could lead to utter failure in another.

In this case there is some indication that the new superintendent is attempting to use the same leadership techniques that have proven successful in other positions. This behavior certainly could be challenged.

OTHER SUGGESTED ACTIVITIES

1. Have the students develop a listing of the merits and pitfalls of trait theories as applied to educational leadership.

2. Have the students develop a list of potential organizational differences between Washington City Schools and the superintendent's previous position (essentially the differences between a small town school district and large metropolitan district).

3. Every organization has formal and informal groups. See if the students can identify such groups in an educational organization in which they are either employees or students.

4. Have students discuss the rights of subordinates to question decisions made by superiors in a school district.

5. Discuss how the superintendent could have approached meeting with the union officials in a more diplomatic manner.

SUGGESTED READINGS:

Bass, B. (1981). *Handbook of leadership: A survey of theory and research.* New York: Free Press.*

Blumberg, A. (1985). A superintendent must read the board's invisible job description. *American School Board Journal,* 172, 44-45.

Castetter, W. (1986). *The personnel function in educational administration* (4th ed.), chaps. 7, 8. New York: Macmillan.

Cuban, L. (1985). Conflict and leadership in the superintendency. *Phi Delta Kappan,* 67, 28-30.

Darling, J., & Ishler, R. (1989/90). Strategic conflict resolution: A problem-oriented approach. *National Forum of Educational Administration and Supervision Journal,* 7(1), 87-103.

Deal, T., & Kennedy, A. (1982). *Corporate cultures.* Reading, MA: Addison-Wesley*

Forrest, J. (1984). The leadership team: Is the strategy working? *Thrust,* 14(1), 29-31.

Gonder, P. (1981). *Collective bargaining: Problems and solutions.* Arlington, VA: American Association of School Administrators.

Guthrie, J., & Reed, R. (1986). *Educational administration and policy,* chap. 12. Englewood Cliffs, NJ: Prentice-Hall.

Hanson, E. (1985). *Educational administration and organizational behavior* (2nd ed.), chap. 3. Boston: Allyn & Bacon.

Hirsch, P., & Andrews, J. (1984). Administrators' response to performance and value challenges: Stance, symbols, and behavior. In T. Sergiovanni & J. Corbally (Eds.), *Leadership and organizational culture,* pp. 171-185. Urbana, IL: University of Illinois Press.

Johnson, S. (1984). *Teacher unions in schools.* Philadelphia, PA: Temple University Press.*

Johnson, S. (1987). Can schools be reformed at the bargaining table. *Teachers College Record,* 89, 269-80.

Johnson, S. (1988). Unionism and collective bargaining in the public schools. In N. Boyan (Ed.), *Handbook of research on educational administration,* pp. 603-622. White Plains, NY: Longman.

Kerchner, C., & Mitchell, D. (1980). *The dynamics of public school collective bargaining and its impacts on governance, administration, and teaching.* Washington, DC: National Institute of Education.

Kowalski, T. (1982). Organizational climate, conflict, and collective bargaining. *Contemporary Education,* 54(1), 27-30.*

Lieberman, M. (1984). Beware of these four fallacies of school system labor relations. *American School Board Journal,* 171(6), 33.

Lieberman, M. (1988). Professional Eithics in Public Education: An Autopsy. *Phi Delta Kappan,* 70(2), 159-160.

Perry, C. (1979). Teacher bargaining: The experience in nine systems. *Industrial and Labor Relations,* 33, 3-17.

Stogdill, R. (1974). *Handbook of leadership: A survey of literature.* New York: Free Press.*

Stuart, L., & Goldschmidt, S. (1985). *Collective bargaining in American public education: The first 25 years.* ERIC, Document Number ED271833.

Yukl, G. (1989). *Leadership in organizations* (2nd ed.), pp.134-135.
  Englewood Cliffs, NJ: Prentice-Hall.

*readings not included in the text

CASE 17

WHO WILL CENSURE THIS BOARD MEMBER?

BACKGROUND INFORMATION

One of the most difficult problems in school administration entails dealing with unethical school board members. Although the national and state organizations for school boards provide codes of ethics, enforcement of these guidelines typically rests with the local community. For example, school board members ought not to become involved in the day-to-day administration of schools. Yet, this frequently occurs and, in some communities, it is even encouraged. Thus, citizen expectations often serve to shape the role for local school board members.

In this case, a board member who is already recognized as a trouble maker attempts to create a problem for one of the high school's athletic programs. The situation is made more complex by virtue of the fact that the board member's action appears to be motivated by a personal consideration--his grandson is the second -string quarterback on the football team. One key facet of this case is the decision the superintendent must make as to whether he should assume the task of censoring the maverick board member.

KEY ISSUES/QUESTIONS

1. *Do you believe that the superintendent is correct in his judgment that Elmer was acting unethically by going to the state athletic association with his complaint?* Two commonly accepted guidelines suggest that the superintendent is correct in his assessment. First, school board members are expected to look to the professional leader of the organization for guidance. This board member made no attempt to address his concerns to the superintendent. Moreover, board members should act in an official capacity only when the school board is in formal decision-making session. Elmer's behavior could be construed as an attempt to abuse his elected office. Yet, the case offers an indication that Elmer did not use his office as leverage when filing his complaint. The official from the athletic association

126

did not discover that he was a school board member until the high school principal relayed this information. Although educational leaders would agree that Elmer acted inappropriately in bypassing the administration and school board with his concern, one should not overlook his rights as a citizen. Should he be expected to conform to a higher standard of ethics because he is on the school board? Can a school board member act as any other citizen when filing complaints against the school system?

2. *Survey school boards in your area and determine if they have policies related to censuring board members for unethical behavior.* Very few school districts maintain a policy regarding this matter. Policies that exist often are vague. Discuss why this condition prevails.

3. *Who should set standards for school board member behavior?* Standards for school board member behavior need to be established at three levels national, state, and local. At the national and state levels, this task is addressed largely through school board associations. At the local level, the school board as an entity under the stewardship of the superintendent should establish policy governing ethical behavior. Local standards may be more specific than state codes and may reflect community standards and expectations. Two factors serve as barriers to establishing local policies on school board member behaviors: (1) board members often cannot agree on such standards, and (2) local citizens view active participation of board members in administration positively.

4. *Do you believe that the superintendent was correct in taking this problem directly to the board president? Would it have been better to talk to Elmer first to get his side of the story?* The case does not reveal what the personal relationship is between Elmer Hodson and Superintendent Karmann. If the two had a positive relationship, going directly to Elmer might have been an acceptable alternative. Not knowing this, the students are likely to support the superintendent's decision to take the matter to the board president. From an organizational perspective, the superintendent appears to have acted appropriately.

5. *Is it ethical or legal for school board members to vote on matters that affect members of their immediate families?* From an

ethical perspective, most students do not believe school board members should vote on matters concerning their own families. Even where such actions are not motivated by personal interests, the public is apt to provide their own interpretation to the situation. From a legal standpoint, laws vary among the fifty states. In a number of states it is illegal for a board member to vote on any matter in which there is the possibility of personal gain. Some states require public officials to file conflict of interest statements. Having local policy on the ethical dimension of this question provides one safeguard against conflict.

6. *Is there an alternative to censuring the board member that the superintendent and board president should consider?* The superintendent and board president ought to consider the advantages and disadvantages of censuring the maverick board member. In addition, they ought to consider talking with him privately to see if they can stress their concerns without creating a public spectacle. A major consideration is what the two leaders want in the way of future relationships with Elmer. By censuring him, they are likely to drive him further away, to make him even less cooperative. Yet, he may be such a bad board member that censure may be the only feasible alternative. If censure becomes the accepted course of action, the board president and superintendent need to decide if they will do this publicly, in an open school board meeting, or privately, in an executive session of the school board. If the concern can be communicated without causing a deeper division on the school board, it should be pursued.

7. *If you were superintendent, would you tell the media about Elmer's behavior? Why or why not?* What is to be gained by taking the matter to media? Do you want to draw more attention to the situation? Given the information in the case, it is difficult to see how publicity would help this situation. Going public would indicate a decision by the board president and superintendent to try to get Elmer off the board.

8. *Determine if your state has provisions for removing school board members from office. If so, what are these provisions?* These provisions vary among the fifty states. It may be helpful to have your students explore if a school board member has been removed from office (recalled) in recent times.

OTHER SUGGESTED ACTIVITIES

1. Invite a panel of school board members from your area to discuss this case in your class. Have them offer opinions about dealing with ethics.

2. Invite an official from the state school board association to visit your class to discuss codes of ethics. How are they formulated, revised, and enforced?

3. Discuss why communities may have differing expectations of school board members.

4. Discuss the advantages of having an appointed rather than elected school board.

5. Discuss the potentiality of athletics to become a major source of conflict for administrators.

SUGGESTED READINGS

Banach, W. (1984). Communications and internal relations are problems for board members. *Journal of Educational Public Relations, 7*(3), 8-9.

Guthrie, J., & Reed, R. (1986). *Educational administration and policy,* pp. 48-55. Englewood Cliffs, NJ: Prentice-Hall.

Hamilton, D. (1987). Healing power: How your board can overcome the heartbreak of disharmony. *American School Board Journal, 174*(9), 36-37.

Hayden, J. (1987). Superintendent-board conflict: Working it out. *Education Digest, 52*(8), 11-13.

Institute for Educational Leadership (1986). *School boards: Strengthening grass roots leadership,* chaps. 8, 9. Washington, DC: Institute for Educational Leadership.

Kowalski, T. (1981). Here's a plan for evaluating your board. *American School Board Journal, 168*(7), 23.

Kowalski, T. (1981). Why your board needs self-evaluation. *American School Board Journal, 168*(7), 21-22.

McDaniel, T. (1986). Learn these rarely written rules of effective board service. *American School Board Journal, 173*(5), 31-32.

Menzies, J. (1986). Power base preferences for resolving conflict: An educational management team consideration. *Journal of Rural and Small Schools*, 1(1), 6-9.

Myer, R. (1983). How to handle a board member who wants to play his own game. *American School Board Journal*, 170(11), 27-29.

Rogers, J. (1988). How to resolve a conflict between board unity and personal integrity. *American School Board Journal*, 175(4), 41-42.*

Simon, T. (1986). *Fundamentals of school board membership*. ERIC, Document Number ED289232.

Wildman, L. (1987). *What can superintendents and board members do to help each other be successful?* ERIC, Document Number ED294312.

Woods, J. (1987). *Internal board of education conflict as compared to Coleman's theory of community conflict*. Unpublished Ed.D. thesis, University of Rochester.

*readings not included in the text

CASE 18

DIFFERING PERCEPTIONS OF TEACHING EFFECTIVENESS

BACKGROUND INFORMATION

This case addresses a positive approach to dealing with conflict. The superintendent attempts to bring parents and educators together to share viewpoints in hopes that they can agree on some objectives for a third-grade class. There are several interesting aspects to this case:

1. The case includes a principal who is dedicated to working toward teacher improvement.

2. The teacher involved has reluctantly accepted a change in assignment at the urging of the principal.

3. This appears to be an affluent community where parents are very concerned about the academic progress of their children.

When students assume the role of the principal, they usually are positive about the action taken by the superintendent. A few students are apt to be critical of her actions, indicating that she should have been more supportive of the professional staff. Also, some students voice concern relative to this solution because they are skeptical that consensus can be reached between the educators and the parents. They see the recommended process as a potential source of additional conflict.

KEY ISSUES/QUESTIONS

1. *Is it common for teachers and parents to have differing perceptions of what schools are to accomplish?* Parents are less apt than teachers to view the affective domain of education as being important. Many parents find it hard to understand why socialization and self-image are goals of public education. Parents usually emphasize the school's role in teaching basic skills and

131

concepts. In this case, some affluent, well-educated parents view affective domain needs as being family responsibilities. They fail to recognize (or chose not to recognize) that the amount of support children receive from families varies significantly. Furthermore, priorities relative to public education, that is, determining what is most important, are not uniform among school districts and professional educators. Within a given school, there may be a myriad of opinions about the primary purposes of schooling and the best ways to achieve those goals. The level of emphasis upon the affective domain goals varies markedly from one school to another.

2. *What factors determine a person's values and beliefs regarding public education?* The values and beliefs of the teachers and administrators are affected by experience as well as formal education. Practitioners see first hand the differing needs of children coming from diverse social and economic backgrounds. Essentially, educators and parents form values and beliefs in a similar fashion. The importance placed on education, religious beliefs, political beliefs, aspirations for children, and social status are but a few of the factors helping to shape individual philosophy.

3. *Do you think that Mrs. Comstock's transfer to third grade is significant in this case?* The case tells us that Mrs. Comstock did not want this assignment; yet, she did not protest. She is probably not happy being in a third-grade assignment. Thus, her attitude concerning her current assignment may be negative. Moreover, the principal probably feels responsible in this situation because he urged her to accept the assignment. Some students correctly point out that expectations for academic work, particularly homework, differ markedly between first and third grade. Mrs. Comstock may be employing practices that worked quite well for her in her previous assignment; but now she finds that they are far less acceptable with older children.

4. *Was it a good decision for the principal not to involve the teacher in the first conference with the parents?* Students tend to give the principal the benefit of doubt in this case. He is viewed as an effective leader and many students conclude that he used good judgment in not having the teacher at the meeting (e.g., he knew she was a fragile person and did not want her to be hurt further by parental complaints). The case does not tell us whether Mrs.

Comstock was consulted relative to whether she wanted to attend this meeting. It is possible that the decision for her not to attend was determined jointly by the principal and teacher. You may wish to pursue the questions of whether the teacher should have been: (1) informed of the meeting, and (2) given an opportunity to decide if she would attend.

5. *Based on what you know from reading this case, do you believe that the principal shares the views of the teacher regarding what is important in education?* It seems the principal's views are closer to the teacher's than to those of the complaining parents. The principal indicates that he believes Mrs. Comstock is doing a reasonably good job and expresses support for the contention that her responsibilities extend beyond teaching the basics. Some students suggest the principal's support for Mrs. Comstock may be related to his feeling that he is responsible for this situation because it was he who transferred her to the third grade.

6. *Could this problem have been averted by stronger interventions on the part of the principal following the initial complaints about homework?* Principals receive many complaints. Some are serious, others are not. Had the principal known initially that the parental complaints would not subside, he may have taken a different course in dealing with the issue. As the instructional leader in the school, the principal has a responsibility to investigate complaints as they are made. If he finds them to be valid, it is expected that corrective action will be taken. If he finds the complaints to be invalid, he has a responsibility to eradicate the misperceptions and to protect the teaching staff from unmerited attacks. After initially receiving complaints, the principal and the teacher agree that more homework will be assigned to the children. This solution apparently sufficed for about six weeks. The resurfacing of the complaints indicates that the treatment of one symptom did not eradicate the problem. In this regard, the principal could be criticized for not directly dealing with the primary source of conflict--differing perceptions between the teacher and some parents regarding the primary goals of this third-grade class.

7. *What are the differences between formative and summative evaluation? Does the fact that the principal views the process as primarily formative have any bearing on this case?* Formative

evaluation is designed to nurture professional growth. Summative evaluation is targeted toward making decisions about reemployment, promotion, or merit salary increases. Given that Mr. Nissaum is concerned with formative evaluation, one would expect that his primary goal is to help teachers rather than to simply make judgments about them. The case also tells us that he spends time working directly with teachers and occasionally assumes the role of instructor when teachers are absent. An orientation toward formative evaluation makes it more difficult to accept parental notions that teachers ought to be categorized, that is, "successful," "outstanding," "below average." Parents may find it difficult to accept the notion that evaluation is designed to promote professional growth.

8. *Assess the superintendent's role in this matter. Was it good practice for her to meet directly with the parents? Should she have made a decision right there in the meeting?* Given the chronology of this case, it is difficult to criticize the actions of the superintendent. In fact, students often praise her actions as being open and purposeful. Moreover, her behavior is applauded because she avoids dictating a decision. Instead, she tries to bring the parties together in hopes that they can find a mutually acceptable solution.

9. *Do you believe that the superintendent's support for the concept of teacher empowerment has any bearing on this case?* Accepting the rights and responsibilities of teachers to make certain professional judgments makes it less likely that the superintendent will be tempted by political alternatives. For example, the easy way out of this situation would be to transfer Mrs. Comstock to another assignment and replace her with a teacher who has a philosophy more congruent with the parents. But such a decision raises at least two major concerns: (1) How would such an action affect community perceptions of the professional role of teachers? (2) Will such a transfer spawn additional requests for similar actions from parents who are dissatisfied with a teacher? Stress the importance of raising such questions as a part of reflective practice.

10. *In what ways does the environment of the community affect this case?* The case does tell us that Rio Del Mar is a growing community. In addition, we know that the particular school in this case is located in an affluent area. Thus, we can surmise that many

of the parents of elementary age children residing in the school area are upward mobiles who place a great deal of emphasis on education. These parents tend to be very concerned about grades, standardized test scores, and similar indices of achievement. When parents view education from this perspective, they tend to be intolerant of practices that do not relate directly to instruction in basic subjects.

11. *What other alternatives could have been pursued by the superintendent in trying to resolve the conflict?* As mentioned earlier, the superintendent could have mandated a transfer of the teacher. Another alternative would have been to require changes in the way the classroom functioned. For instance, the principal could have been directed to make more observations to assure that parental concerns were being addressed. Another option would have been to side totally with the teacher. If this were done, the superintendent would declare that the teacher was doing a good job and that the parents were interfering in professional judgments. None of these alternatives appears to be better than the one actually pursued by the superintendent.

12. *Is the superintendent correct in her assessment that conflict can lead to positive outcomes?* Organizational theorists point out that conflict is neither good nor bad. Its final value depends on the manner in which it is managed. Conflict often leads to change and organizational change can be positive. For instance, this case could result in closer working relationships, better communication, and so forth between the school and parents. You may want to develop a list of potential positive outcomes.

13. *Evaluate the behavior of the principal in the January meeting he had with parents. Was he effective? What would you have done differently if you were in his place?* The principal attempted to be candid with the parents regarding his position on Mrs. Comstock. Meeting with a group of angry parents is a task most principals do not cherish. The meeting accomplished one thing--the parties were able to communicate their feelings. Clearly, the meeting did not resolve the grievance. For this reason, some students conclude that the meeting was not effective. This conclusion may be a bit unfair. Often grievances require a number of steps before a suitable resolution is established. Short of giving in to the parents, it is difficult to see how the principal could have behaved differently.

135

OTHER SUGGESTED ACTIVITIES

1. Have a professor in foundations of education visit your class to discuss why individuals often differ markedly in their philosophies of education.

2. Discuss the merits of providing parents with detailed objectives at the beginning of a school year as an attempt to avoid problems such as the one presented in this case.

3. Discuss how this case may relate to school site management.

4. Review the effects of educational reform efforts on parental perceptions of what should be expected from public schools.

SUGGESTED READINGS:

Beckham, J. (1985). Legally sound criteria, processes, and procedures for the evaluation of public school professional employees. *Journal of Law and Education*, 14(4), 529-551.

Bullock, W., & Davis, J. (1985). Interpersonal factors that influence principals' ratings of teacher performance. *Planning and Changing*, 16(1), 3-11.

Castetter, W. (1986). *The personnel function in educational administration* (4th ed.), chap. 15. New York: Macmillan.

Epstein, J. (1985). A question of merit: Principals' and parents' evaluations of teachers. *Educational Researcher*, 14(7), 3-10.

Epstein, J. (1988). Parents and schools: How do we improve programs for parent involvement? *Educational Horizons*, 66(3), 59-95.

Glassman, N. (1985). Perceptions of school principals about their engagement in evaluation on the basis of student data. *Studies in Educational Evaluation*, 11(2), 231-236.

Hawley, R. (1982). *Assessing teacher performance*. Amherst, MA: Education Research Associates.*

Margolis, H., & Tewel, K. (1988). Resolving conflict with parents: A guide for administrators. *NASSP Bulletin*, 72(506), 26-28.

Medley, D., & Coker, H. (1987). The accuracy of principals' judgements of teacher performance. *Journal of Educational Research*, 80(4), 242-247.

Medley, D., Coker, H., & Soar, R. (1984). *Measurement-based evaluation of teacher performance,* pp.14-23. NewYork: Longman

Minex, N., et al. (1986). *Development of a goal setting process and instrumentation for teachers and principals.* ERIC, Document Number 290796.

Moo, G. (1987). Communicating with the school publics. *NASSP Bulletin,* 71(501), 142-144.

Oliva, P. (1984). *Supervision for today's schools* (2nd ed.), pp. 156-205. New York: Longman.*

Peterson, D. (1983). Legal and ethical issues of teacher evaluation: A research based approach. *Educational Research Quarterly,* 7(4), 6-16.

Redinger, L. (1988). *Evaluation: A means of improving teacher performance.* ERIC, Document Number ED299231.

Ross, V. (1984). We use standardized student test scores to rate teachers. *Executive Educator,* 6(3), 22-23.

Sapone, C. (1982). Appraisal and evaluation systems: What are the perceptions of educators, board members? *NASSP Bulletin,* 66(458), 46-51.

Spillane, R. (1989). The changing principalship:A superintendent's perspective. *Principal,* 68(3), 19-20.

Snyder, K., & Anderson, R. (1986). *Managing productive schools: Toward an ecology,* chap. 8. Orlando, FL: Academic Press College Division.

Stinnett, T., & Henson, K. (1982). *America's public schools in transition,* chap. 5. New York: Teachers College Press.*

Trentman, L., et al. (1985). Teacher efficacy and teacher competency ratings. *Psychology in the Schools,* 22(3), 343-352.

Wall, T. (1984). *The illusions of independence in evaluation.* ERIC, Document Number ED292831.

Wood, C., Nicholson, E., & Findley, D. (1985). *The secondary school principal* (2nd ed.), pp. 148-174. Boston: Allyn & Bacon.

Zirkel, P. (1985). Defamation for educator evaluation. *NASSP Bulletin,* 69(477), 90-92.

*readings not included in the text

CASE 19

TRYING TO PREVENT UNIONIZATION

BACKGROUND INFORMATION

The acceptance of collective bargaining in school districts has not been uniform across the United States. In this case, a long-term superintendent threatens to retire immediately if the school board rejects his recommendation to deny union recognition for noncertificated staff (secretaries, custodians, etc.). The superintendent's objections to unionization are so strong that he is willing to take this drastic measure.

Over the twenty-four years this person has served as superintendent, he has established a number of friendships and many staff members and residents of the community are loyal to him. Several other noteworthy factors in this case include: (1) the general attitude of the community toward collective bargaining; (2) the approach to problem solving that is used between the superintendent and the board (they try to use political leverage); (3) the uncertainty of the school board relative to how the central office staff will react if the superintendent resigns; and (4) the difficult position in which an elementary principal is placed by the three board members.

THE CHALLENGE

Many aspiring administrators believe that job opportunities are largely a matter of luck. That is, they see many educational leaders getting good jobs simply because they are in the right place at the right time. For these students, there is a tremendous temptation to seize the opportunity presented to the elementary principal in this case. They argue that to get ahead in the profession, one must be willing to take risks and to capitalize on opportunities as they occur.

More cautious students raise a number of questions about responding to the invitation to become acting superintendent.

Consider the following:
1. What would happen if the principal says yes to the three board members and then the superintendent does not resign? Even more importantly, what would happen if the superintendent discovers that the principal engaged in these secret conversations?

2. Would accepting the offer create an image among board members that the principal would be willing to do almost anything to get a better job?

3. How would the community react if the superintendent quit and the principal became acting superintendent? Could it turn out to be an impossible job?

4. Is it ethical to consider such offers under the conditions discribed in the case?

KEY ISSUES/QUESTIONS

1. *Does the fact that Curtis has been superintendent a long time affect the way that you would react if you were Mrs. Kendrick?* Most students will recognize that long-term superintendents are more likely to have political power in the community. As such, the risk is greater for Mrs. Kendrick in this case. If she agrees to cooperate with the three school board members, she may suffer some political negatives stemming from loyalties to Curtis. You should point out the importance of superintendents and other administrators understanding power relationships within a community. Many supporters of the current superintendent are apt to accuse Mrs. Kendrick of being part of a conspiracy.

2. *Why do you believe Curtis is so opposed to collective bargaining?* Over his twenty-four-year tenure as superintendent and during his professional career prior to this appointment, Curtis experienced many changes in public education. Individuals, including administrators, exhibit different levels of adaptation. A sizable number of superintendents in the U.S. found it particularly difficult to accept collective bargaining. Some rejected unionization because they saw it as an erosion of administrative authority. Others objected because they were convinced it would create more problems than it

139

would solve. But there are others who understood the reasons why bargaining existed and attempted to find success with the process.

3. *What political dimensions affect the way in which school board members react to this request for collective bargaining rights?* Individual board members may be affected by personal beliefs as well as political considerations. In this case, for instance, there is at least the suggestion that the board president is concerned about how his vote will affect customers in the bank where he is employed. Board members who also are in private business frequently become concerned about negative economic repercussions of policy decisions. Beyond economic concerns, board members also may be persuaded to vote in a certain fashion because of friendships or family interests (e.g., a board member who has a relative who is in the group seeking union recognition).

4. *Myron Lieberman argues that school board members do not always make good decisions related to collective bargaining because they can leave office to avoid the consequences of poor decisions. Do you agree or disagree with this judgment?* Lieberman was once a primary advocate for collective bargaining in public education. Over the years, he has changed his position entirely. He now contends that public boards of control often make poor decisions in collective bargaining for which they are rarely held accountable. Students tend to disagree on whether he is correct. Students who may have had an active role in collective bargaining while they were teachers are especially prone to reject Lieberman's contention. The successes and failures of collective bargaining across the U. S. makes it difficult to generalize on this question. Some school districts may not have offered any avenue to teachers for dealing with conflict. In these instances, collective bargaining may have produced some positive outcomes. In other situations, the process may have created unusually high levels of conflict.

5. *Assess the superintendent's strategy in sending the letter threatening resignation to the board. Was it ethical? Was it politically sound?* Knowledgeable practitioners agree that the move on the part of the superintendent was myopic. Even if he succeeds, he is apt to create ill feelings and to delay the issue for two years (until he retires). The process of trying to coerce your opponents into doing something they do not want to do is a common practice in

political circles. It is not, however, the best way to solve differences. Exercising power via threat is a practice that soon loses its potency. A superintendent can do this only a certain number of times before opponents rebel.

6. *Assess the behavior of the three board members who met secretly at Huffman's house. Was it ethical? Was it politically sound?* School board members are not supposed to conduct business outside of official meetings of the board as a whole. In this regard, their action was unethical. Politically, they are trying to outsmart the superintendent. In essence, both parties are engaging in a political chess match. Given the importance of the issue, neither party is really doing the right thing. In some states, their activity (having secret meetings, taking straw votes) may raise legal questions because they: (1) constitute a majority of the board, and (2) are making promises on behalf of the entire board.

7. *What steps could be taken in this district to improve superintendent and school board relationships?* Both parties need to understand accepted roles for boards of education and superintendents. The superintendent should realize that his job is to make recommendations and to provide background data to support the recommendations. If a majority of the board rejects his recommendation, his obligation is to formulate a new recommendation. In this case, both sides are trying to manipulate rather than to deal with the differences in an open fashion. You want to draw a linkage between the superintendent's dislike of unions and his own proclivity to avoid compromise.

8. *What factors should be weighed by the board in reaching a decision of whether to recognize the union for purposes of collective bargaining?* The most common responses include the following: (1) Finding out whether these employees have ways of becoming involved in key decisions that affect them; (2) determining what human and economic resources will be required if the union is recognized; (3) determining whether the community supports the notion of permitting collective bargaining for these employees; and (4) determining whether similar situations in other school districts have proven to be successful or unduly burdensome.

9. *What is meant by "Right to Work State?" Are school boards in your state required to collectively bargain with all employees?* A right to work state does not allow any laws or agreements that makes employment contingent on union membership. States have varying laws, so students should determine the status of right to work in your state.

OTHER SUGGESTED ACTIVITIES

1. Discuss the ethical issues raised for the principal in this case.

2. Ask students what additional information they would like to have had with relation to the principal.

3. Have students explore the literature for explanations for the use of unionization and collective bargaining in education.

SUGGESTED READINGS:

Boehm, R., & Heldman, D. (1982). *Public employees, unions, and the erosion of public trust: A study of San Francisco in the 1970s.* Frederick, MD: University Publications of America.*

Botan, H., & Frey, L. (1983). Do workers trust labor unions and their messages? *Communication Monographs, 50,* 233-244.

Castetter, W. (1986). *The personnel function in educational administration* (4th ed.), chap. 7. New York: Macmillan.

Christensen, S. (1980). *Unions and the public interest: Collective bargaining in the government sector.* Vancouver, BC: Fraser Institute.*

Goldschmidt, S., & Painter, S. (1988). Collective Bargaining: A Review of the Literature. *Educational Research Quarterly, 12*(1), 10-24.

Guthrie, J., & Reed, R. (1986). *Educational administration and policy,* chap. 12. Englewood Cliffs, NJ: Prentice-Hall.

Hanson, E. (1985). *Educational administration and organizational behavior* (2nd ed.), chap. 3. Boston: Allyn & Bacon.

Helsby, R. (1979). A political system for a political world--In public sector labor relations. In M. Levine & E. Hagburg (Eds), *Labor relations in the public sector*, pp. 46-55. Salt Lake City, UT: Brighton Publishing.*

Kearny, R. (1983). Public employment, public employer unions, and the 1980s. *School Library Media Quarterly*, 11, 269-278.

Kennedy, J. (1984). When collective bargaining first came to education: A superintendent's viewpoint. *Government Union Review*, 5(1), 14-26.

Kerchner, C. (1978). From scopes to scope: The genetic mutation of the school control issue. *Educational Administration Quarterly*, 14(1) 64-79.

Kerchner, C., & Mitchell, D. (1980). *The dynamics of public school collective bargaining and its impacts on governance, administration, and teaching.* Washington, DC: National Institute of Education.

Kowalski, T. (1982). Organizational climate, conflict, and collective bargaining. *Contemporary Education,* 54(1), 27-30.

Lieberman, M. (1979). Eggs I have laid: Teacher bargaining reconsidered. *Phi Delta Kappan*, 60, 415-419.

Lieberman, M. (1984). Beware of these four common fallacies of school system labor relations. *American School Board Journal*, 171(6), 33.

Lieberman, M. (1986). *Beyond public education*, pp. 19-44. New York: Praeger.

Nyberg, D. (1990). Power, empowerment, and educational authority. In S. Jacobson & J. Conway (Eds.), *Educational Leadership in an age of reform*, pp. 47-64. New York: Longman.*

Rebore, R. (1984). *A handbook for school board members,* chap. 1. Englewood Cliffs, NJ: Prentice-Hall.

Shedd, J. (1988). Collective bargaining, school reform and the management of school systems. *Educational Administration Quarterly*, 24(4), 405-415.

Staw, B. (1984). Leadership and persistence. In T. Sergiovanni & J. Corbally (Eds.), *Leadership and organizational culture*, pp. 72-84. Urbana, IL: University of Illinois Press.

Tyler, G. (1976). Why they organize. In A. Cresswell & M. Murphy (Eds.), *Education and collective bargaining*, pp. 12-21. Berkeley, CA: McCutchan.*

143

Van Hook, B. (1987). *Clerical workers and organized labor: Preservice educational imperatives.* ERIC, Document Number EJ351861.*

*readings not included in the text

CASE 20

LET'S NOT RAP

KEY ISSUES/QUESTIONS

Case 20 exemplifies how several controversial issues can converge to create a most difficult problem. Convocations in urban high schools are rather common. In this case, an attempt to present a drug prevention message is embroiled in controversy because of accusations of antisemitism toward the black performing group invited to do a convocation. The situation is exacerbated by the presence of a parental group that has been complaining about insensitivity toward blacks in the school. The principal is caught between conflicting demands coming from two parental groups.

Students typically exhibit strong disagreement over this case. This is especially true if your class includes students who identify with either parental/student group cited in the case. Some students may suggest that they would attempt to bring the two parental groups together. This is a difficult path to follow because the Parents Advocating Racial Awareness (PARA) is a formal group within the school/community and no parallel group exists for the Jewish parents (at least the case makes no mention of such a group). Additionally, time parameters become an issue in trying to bring the two groups to some type of compromise. The convocation is scheduled for a specific date and that leaves little time for discussion.

1. *Do you think the principal should have handled this matter differently when approached by the student to have the convocation?* Any time celebrities or political leaders are invited to do a convocation in a public school, there is the possibility that some person or group will object. For this reason, it is highly advisable to do a rather extensive background check on groups or individuals who will be making presentations. It would have been to the principal's advantage to do this prior to making a verbal commitment to the student. Although this more cautious approach may not have totally eliminated the problem, it would have made it more manageable.

145

2. *Do you think that the activities of the student's father had anything to do with the principal's behavior?* The existence of the PARA group is a critical factor in this case. The principal probably is very sensitive to the fact that this group is already complaining about mistreatment of black students. This prevailing condition almost certainly would affect the principal's behavior. Problems must be examined in relation to existing conditions. The perception of mistreatment of blacks is certainly a cogent condition.

3. *Should schools ever allow persons to speak to students if their views are contrary to the values and beliefs embraced by the community?* Among the many difficult decisions a principal must make, allowing controversial speakers to use the school as a platform for ideas is one of the most perplexing. Many authorities advocate providing a balance of viewpoints when such situations occur. There are instances, however, where the message is so offensive to the community that many authorities argue that the views simply should not be expressed under the sanction of the school (e.g., someone advocating militant revolution). There is a legal and a political dimension to this question. The school district attorney should become involved in the former.

4. *What are the advantages and disadvantages of cancelling the program?* No matter what the principal does, one group will be angry. The decision should be based on what the administration believes to be morally correct. The superintendent presents a cogent question in the case when he asks how the principal would react if it were a Jewish group making negative comments about blacks. By permitting the convocation to occur, the principal is risking the formation of yet another parental pressure group. By cancelling it, she is likely to intensify negative feelings among the black students. One suggested option in relation to cancelling would be to invite student leaders representing all ethnic and religious groups to participate in a series of discussions about this incident. The principal could use the conflict surrounding the convocation as a catalyst to promote multicultural education and better understanding of varying values and beliefs within the school.

5. *What do you anticipate the repercussions will be if the program is cancelled?* If the program is simply cancelled and nothing else is done, it is probable that the black students and parents will feel that

they are again the losers. It would be a mistake to simply make a decision on the convocation and do nothing else. Without an explanation, it is likely that various motives will emerge in the minds of students and parents.

6. *Anticipate the repercussions if the program is not cancelled.* As mentioned previously, allowing the convocation to go on as planned could result in the Jewish parents forming their own pressure group. It also could spawn legal action by some of the parents or national Jewish organizations.

7. *What are your impressions of Dr. Tolliver, the superintendent? Do you approve of his behavior in this case? What would you do differently if you were superintendent?* Some students criticize the superintendent because they prefer a leader who would give specific directions to the principal. Other students praise the superintendent for allowing his staff to assume responsibility for critical decisions. This question offers an excellent opportunity to discuss how individuals in the principalship develop differing role expectations of their supervisors. Some principals prefer to work in highly structured environments; others prefer to have high degrees of freedom in executing responsibilities.

8. *Prepare a statement that you would read or send to students announcing your decision (i.e., to either cancel or not cancel).* The key element with this directive is to see whether students have the foresight to deal with the issue beyond either cancelling or permitting it to go on as planned. Creative leaders will seize the opportunity to use this incident for educational purposes. Also, some students see this issue as symptomatic of a larger problem (a lack of sensitivity, a lack of understanding about different cultures).

9. *What is more important to a school like Roosevelt, fighting drugs or fighting racism?* Most students react that both goals are important and must be addressed by the school. Some will argue that racism is more important because it is a more difficult problem and pervasive condition in our society. This question is perplexing; yet, it is essentially the primary query that the principal had to answer.

OTHER SUGGESTED ACTIVITIES

1. Many graduate students, especially those who may have been reared in rural locations, have had little exposure to other cultures and religions prior to attending college. For this reason, it may be a good idea to have an extended discussion on the importance of multicultural education.

2. Invite leaders from organizations (e.g., black or Jewish groups) to your class to discuss the ramifications of this case.

3. Invite an attorney to discuss how laws in your state would affect this case.

4. Assign students the task of formulating a regulation that would prevent this type of situation from recurring.

SUGGESTED READINGS:

Drake, T., & Roe, W. (1986). *The principalship* (3rd ed.) chap. 7. New York: Macmillan.

Harker, R. (1981). *Multiculturalism and multicultural schools.* ERIC, Document Number ED225775.

Hollen, G. (1984). School assemblies as supplements to classroom learning. *NASSP Bulletin*, 68(472), 134-135.

Hoy, W., & Forsyth, P. (1986). *Effective supervision: Theory into practice,* chap. 7. New York: Random House.

Kowalczewski, P. (1982). Race and education: Racism, diversity, and inequality implications for multicultural education. *Oxford Review of Education*, 8(2), 145-161.

Margolis, H., & Tewel, K. (1988). Resolving conflict with parents: A guide for administrators. *NASSP Bulletin*, 72(506), 26-28.

McLeer, J. (1983). Understanding anti-semitism. *Curriculum Review*, 22, 99.

Pate, G. (1988). Research on reducing prejudice. *Social Education*, 52, 287-289.

Reiharz, J. (Ed.) (1987). *Living with antisemitism: Modern Jewish responses.* Hanover, NH: Brandeis University Press & University Press of New England.*

Tobin, G. (1988). *Jewish perceptions of antisemitism.* New York: Plenum Press.*

Valverde, L. (1988). Principals creating better schools in minority communities. *Education and Urban Society,* 2(4), 319-326.

Valverde, L. (1988). Principals embracing cultural reality. *Teacher Education & Practice,* 4(1), 47-51.

Wood, C., Nicholson, E., & Findley, D. (1985). *The secondary school principal: Manager and supervisor* (2nd ed.), chap. 10. Boston: Allyn & Bacon.

Zirkel, P., & Gluckman, I. (1983). Stop, don't raise that curtain. *NASSP Bulletin,* 62(463), 110-112.

*readings not included in the text

CASE 21

WHO DECIDES STANDARDS FOR EMPLOYING A PRINCIPAL?

BACKGROUND INFORMATION

Although conflict exists in all organizations, it is more prevelant in some institutions than in others. In Case 21, we find a school district where conflict, at least overt conflict, has been rather rare. The presence of two new board members seems to be changing that fact.

Students find this to be a challenging case. Consider some of the more salient points: (1) the superintendent is well-respected by the veteran board members, especially the board president; (2) in the past, the board appears to have been very oriented toward supporting management; (3) the board has established a separation between policy making and administration. As the two new board members question procedures relative to employment practices for principals, two veteran board members seem to side with them, indicating that some change may be in order.

The superintendent must evaluate the importance of the matter and determine if the two new board members merely want to review standards or whether this request is associated with broader concerns. Oftentimes administrators become inflexible over matters that are not critical or they blindly protect past practices. Two initiatives are cogent: (1) the superintendent needs to determine if the procedures can be improved and to act accordingly, and (2) he needs to determine if the questioning signals a change in thinking on the part of the board members.

KEY ISSUES/CHALLENGES

1. *Identify options available to the superintendent. Evaluate each.*
   a. The superintendent could stand firm on the position that employment is a management prerogative and that he is not obligated to listen to teachers. The possible advantages include the protection of power and the creation of a situation

150

where compromise is not necessary (i.e., the superintendent alone will determine the qualifications). The disadvantages include the possible alienation of some board members and the perception that the superintendent is inflexible.

b. The superintendent could permit the board to dictate the standards and conditions. There is a possible advantage because board members may like to have greater involvement in such areas. There may also be a disadvantage because such action is a non-management solution. That is, the superintendent is merely abdicating his responsibilities in order to remove the conflict.

c. The superintendent could solicit input from teachers and others and then assess the qualifications based on those suggestions. There is the advantage that this assessment activity is likely to produce the most accurate needs information. Furthermore, the superintendent will be exhibiting that he is a flexible individual. However, this option is going to be more time consuming and require compromise, which may possibly be a disadvantage.

2. Do you think it is good or bad that board meetings in Carrollton rarely last longer than ninety minutes? In our society, we have a proclivity to make judgments based solely on efficiency. The time duration of board meetings is not the only issue to be weighed. How is this time used? Are the board meetings democratic? It is possible to conduct very good meetings in one hour and to have absolutely terrible meetings that last for six or more hours. The answer to this question rests with the effectiveness of the board meetings. If the work is being done and if the meetings are functioning in a democratic manner, the duration of the meetings might be very appropriate.

3. Is it common for new school board members to challenge the status quo? New members often are reluctant to speak out in their first months on the school board. Increasingly, however, individuals run for a school board office on a platform advocating change. For these individuals, the first meeting may not be soon enough to voice objections, opinions, and the like. General conditions in the environment have an effect on board members. Environments can be rather calm (i.e., free of turmoil) or stormy (i.e., conditions where change is desired and demanded). In the era of educational

151

reform, board members, including new ones, are more likely to challenge the status quo. In many communities, candidates form slates, openly advocating radical changes (e.g., dismissing the superintendent).

4. *Should teachers have some input regarding the qualifications for principals in their school?* Any time a question challenges traditional management practices, it can be expected that students will exhibit disagreement. With the advent of teacher empowerment, it is likely that teachers will become increasingly involved in such matters. It may be helpful for you to point out the differences related to teachers helping to set criteria and their actual involvement in the search and selection processes. If a school system is trying to improve instruction, creating effective relationships between principals and teachers is a step in that direction. Forward thinking leaders are exploring ways to infuse collaborative decision processes into the school.

5. *Should teachers ever be allowed to interview candidates for the principalship?* This query is similar to item 4, yet it is distinctively different. Involvement of teachers in the interviews does not mean that they will be voting participants in the decision. The superintendent could seek their input in an advisory capacity. Therefore, you should be clear about the conditions (voting or simply input) in assessing student responses to this item. Most leaders are more prone to permitting input in interviews rather than a role in selection decisions. You may wish to question students who are negative about teacher involvement relative to their reasons for taking this stance.

6. *Do you think Mr. Reller, the board president, was trying to protect the superintendent?* Protecting the superintendent is one possibility. The following are two other possibilities that merit considerations: (1) the board president may have been protecting his own power on the board when he objected to members challenging his rulings, and (2) the board president may be protecting practices in which he feels a sense of ownership (the existing policies). We know from the information provided that Mr. Reller is an account executive. It is possible that he is applying values prevalent in his work life to his role as school board president. But again, the information is inconclusive.

152

7. *How could this confrontation have been avoided?* In all probability, this situation could have been avoided if the superintendent would have been willing to suggest that the issue was worth discussion. His mode of responding may have been interpreted negatively by the new board members. If they perceive him to be evasive, this may account for their persistence. Simply saying that "this is the way we have always done it" is not apt to satisfy the inquiring school board members. Neither avoidance nor arrogance is apt to produce a desirable outcome.

8. *Several board members view conflict as inefficient. Give some possible explanations for their judgment.* The view that conflict is inefficient comes from bureaucratic notions and values about organizations. Often, individuals fail to weigh the significance of schools having to operate in the public domain. All organizations are unique, but public organizations are substantially different from private institutions. They are expected to create linkages and interactions. Conflict is more likely in public organizations.

9. *Do you think it is likely that this school board will now have split votes on many issues? Why or why not?* In part, the answer to this question rests with the way the superintendent and board president decide to handle the matter. If they approach the situation in a flexible manner, the other board members may look favorably on their behavior. If they are inflexible, they are more likely to push the questioning board members into an adversarial position. As stated earlier, we do not know if the questioning of employment practices signals a change in board philosophy or practices. It may be an isolated incident.

OTHER SUGGESTED ACTIVITIES

1. Invite a board president to your class to give his or her perspective on this case. If possible, also invite a representative from your state school board association.

2. Discuss how reform efforts in public education are contributing to a different perspective on the principalship.

3. Discuss teacher empowerment and the potential ramifications related to the selection of administrators.

SUGGESTED READINGS:

Abbott, M., & Caracheo, F. (1988). Power, authority, and bureaucracy. In N. Boyan (Ed.), *Handbook of research on educational administration,* pp. 239-258. White Plains, NY: Longman.

Black, J., & English, F. (1986). *What they don't tell you in schools of education about school administration,* chap. 12. Lancaster, PA: Technomic.

Castetter, W. (1986). *The personnel function in educational administration* (4th ed.), chap. 9. New York: Macmillan.

Connelly, F., & Clandinin, D. (1984). *The role of teachers personal practical knowledge in effecting board policy.* ERIC, Document Number ED271535.

Dow, I. (1983). The effect of school management patterns on organizational effectiveness. *Alberta Journal of Educational Research,* 29(1), 31-45.

Drake, T., & Roe, W. (1986). *The principalship* (3rd ed.), chap. 8. New York: Macmillan.

Fullen, M. (1983). *Change processes and strategies at the local level.* ERIC, Document Number ED245358.

Harris, B. (1985). *Personnel administration in education: Leadership for instructional improvement.* Boston: Allyn & Bacon.*

Heller, R., & Pautler, A. (1990). The administrator of the future: Combining instructional and managerial leadership. In S. Jacobson & J. Conway (Eds.), *Educational leadership in an age of reform,* pp. 131-143. New York: Longman.*

Ibla, R. (1987). Defining the big principal--What schools and teachers want in their leaders. *NASSP Bulletin,* 71(500), 94-98.

Immegart, G. (1988). Leadership and leader behavior. In N. Boyan(Ed.), *Handbook of research on educational administration,* pp. 259- 278. White Plains, NY: Longman.

Institute for Educational Leadership (1986). *School boards: Strengthening grass roots leadership.* Washington, DC: Institute for Educational Leadership.*

Kaufman, R. (1983). A holistic planning model: A system approach for improving organizational effectiveness and impact. *Performance and Instruction,* 22(8), 3-12.

Lawler, E. (1985). Education, management style, and organizational effectiveness. *Personnel Psychology,* 38(1), 1-26.

Schon, D. (1983). *The reflective practitioner,* chaps. 1, 2. New York: Basic Books.

Sloan, C., & Del-Bene, D. (1983). The perceptions of elementary school principals. *Journal of the Association for the Study of Perception,* 18(1) 11-14.

Trump, J. (1986). *What hinders or prevents secondary school principals from being instructional leaders?* ERIC, Document Number ED284365.

Wood, C., Nicholson, E., & Findley, D. (1985). *The secondary school principal: Manager and supervisor* (2nd ed.), chap. 9. Boston: Allyn & Bacon.

Yukl, G. (1989). *Leadership in organizations* (2nd ed.), pp 23-33, chap. 3. Englewood Cliffs, NJ: Prentice-Hall.

*readings not included in text

"NARC" OR SOCIAL WORKER? OR MAYBE EDUCATIONAL LEADER?

BACKGROUND INFORMATION

This case profiles a female principal who takes a risk by establishing an in-school suspension program to deal with drug abuse problems. Several key topics emerge, including the following: (1) the conditions under which she acquired the job; (2) her husband's attitude toward her job; (3) her apparent trust in her immediate supervisor; (4) her willingness to make bold decisions; and (5) her level of experience in administration prior to taking the job. There are several indicators in the case study that the in-school suspension program is not working well (e.g., far more students are involved than was anticipated). Also, negative views of the concept are being reinforced by publicity about the program. Failures, not successes, are being illuminated.

In responding to this situation, you should encourage students to place the program (in-school suspension) in the context of the school and the specific level of drug use occurring there. Often students believe that programs can be equally successful in all environments. The information provided here raises serious questions as to whether this program should survive. The key problem-solving issue is the ability of the students to weigh all of the circumstances surrounding this situation; their ability to establish and evaluate alternative responses; and their willingness to make a decision about the future of the program.

KEY ISSUES/QUESTIONS

1. *Do you think Pat was prepared to become principal of this school? Why or why not?* Many students will likely respond that Pat was not really prepared to assume this position. Why? Many will judge that she should have been an assistant principal prior to assuming her current post. Career patterns, especially for women administrators, frequently do not follow the prescribed paths

common among males. The fact that Pat may have moved directly to the principalship may not be that unusual for a female. The primary focus relative to experience should be placed on the quality of experiences, regardless of the type of position held while acquiring these experiences. Having worked as a coordinator of English education, Pat's role with teachers was primarily in a consultant capacity. As principal, she encounters differing role expectations. The case provides clues, for instance, that she was somewhat naive about how she could spend her time as a principal. You may wish to point out that principals with tremendously different leadership styles often achieve high levels of success.

2. *Was it a good idea to appoint a committee to recommend what should be done about substance abuse problems?* Many professionals agree that drug abuse is a problem that must be addressed on several fronts. In this regard, engaging professionals in the study of the problem was a good decision. Furthermore, some students defend Pat's action on the basis that shared decision making is a healthy process for public education. Individuals prone to defending closed climates will disagree with her actions. They are more likely to see the committee as a disruptive force creating conflict. Critics of contemporary education practices frequently lament that school officials do not fully utilize community resources to solve problems.

3. *What is your impression of the behavior of the three assistant principals in this case?* Although each of the assistants was willing to become principal, and although each stated opposition to Pat's plans to establish an in-school suspension program, the case provides no information to indicate that they were responsible for the bad publicity or other problems plaguing the program. Any impressions students may formulate are largely based on abstractions. Some students may comment that the assistant principals are offering sound advice to the principal.

4. *Do you think that Pat's family situation has any bearing on this case? If so, in what respect?* No individual can totally separate personal life from professional life. The fact that Pat's husband did not want her to become a high school principal and the fact that she is now encountering a major problem in that job are significant. The family considerations are likely to have more bearing on whether she

157

remains in the principalship as opposed to whether she continues the suspension program. Individual administrators vary markedly in the weight they place on family life in making career decisions. Thus, you can expect some students to emphasize the spouse's views, whereas others will see family considerations as relatively unimportant. This question also provides an opportunity to discuss stresses unique to female administrators who are married.

5. *What are the advantages and disadvantages of in-school suspension programs?* Advocates of in-school suspension argue that the program provides the best educational and disciplinary solution to drug problems in schools. They contend that removal from the school environment (suspension) punishes parents more than students and simply makes it likely that the students will eventually drop out of school. Critics note that certain students should not be allowed to remain in school because their transgressions present a danger or impediment to the normal functions of the school. Furthermore, they posit that in-school suspension represents only token discipline and is not taken seriously by the students. In-school suspensions remain a topic of controversy in public education. Direct your students to the literature if you want to probe deeper into this issue.

6. *Is the size of the school an important consideration in this case?* When two factors are taken into consideration, the total size of the school and the overcrowding in the program, it is reasonable to conclude that the size of the school is a factor in the case. For example, the principal may have been better off restricting the in-school suspension to very minor offenses or first offenders. Or, maybe she should have created two separate programs for a school this size. Also, we do not know if adequate resources (rooms, faculty, counselors) were available to assure desired levels of operation.

7. *Do you think Dr. Javier gave Pat good advice?* Dr. Javier gives Pat advice at two points in this case. First, he tells her that the creation of the program was really her decision. Then once problems occur, he tells her that she should not leave her job simply because of this problem. In the first instance, he could be criticized. Given that the principal was quite inexperienced, it is reasonable to expect that he would have been more directive and helpful in advising her on whether to establish the suspension program. By

simply telling her it was her decision, he offered no direction. The advice he gave her later is more acceptable.

8. *What alternatives could Pat have pursued instead of the in-school suspension program?* The case tells us that there was an intention to change selected procedures at the high school, but there is no direct evidence that these changes included disciplinary procedures. Therefore, one alternative that Pat could have followed would have been to maintain the programs already in place (regular suspensions and expulsions). Another option would have been to suspend the students from school but to require their participation in an alternative school program during this period. A third consideration entails a requirement to seek counseling during the suspension period (e.g., from mental health clinics).

9. *Do you think school administrators receive adequate academic preparation to deal with problems such as the one in this case?* High school principals have varying levels of education and experience. They differ in degree level, experience prior to becoming a principal, and curricular experiences encountered in graduate school (i.e., not all universities require the same curriculum for becoming a principal). On average, individuals assuming the principalship have little preparation in dealing with substance abuse problems. Inservice education has become a primary source of information.

10. *Do you think the school district should have specific policies governing the operation of in-school suspension program?* Some individuals prefer to work in organizations dominated by rules and regulations. Others desire to work in a setting where there is room for self-determination. Students who fall into the former group will answer this question in the affirmative; the other group is likely to oppose specific policy for the program.

11. *Do you think that women face special problems in the secondary principalship?* Women in school administration are most likely to be found in two positions: (1) the elementary principalship, and (2) central office staff positions (e.g., curriculum coordinator). The high school principalship has been dominated by males, many of whom come from backgrounds in coaching. Athletics often play a key role in high schools, thus this condition is not surprising. As more women enter administration and as high schools place greater

159

emphasis on academics, the barriers to women should become less severe. It is possible that some will associate gender with this problem. Such linkages usually result from prejudice or stereotypes and not empirical data.

OTHER SUGGESTED ACTIVITIES

1. See if your students can identify how many female high school principals there are in your state. See if you can arrange for one of them to visit the class to discuss this case.

2. Identify in-school suspension programs in your state. Obtain information relative to their operations and their levels of success.

3. Invite experts in drug abuse and student discipline procedures to your class to discuss this case.

SUGGESTED READINGS:

Buscemi, M. (1985). What schools are doing to prevent alcohol and drug abuse. *The School Administrator*, 4(9), 11-14.
Daria, R. (1987). Remedy for drug abuse: Honesty, discipline, help for troubled students. *American School Board Journal*, 174(8), 37, 54.
Dean, O. (1989). *Facing chemical dependency in the classroom with student assistance programs*. Deerfield Beach, FL: Health Communications.*
Edson, S. (1981). *Female aspirants to public school administration: Why do they continue to aspire to principalships?* Unpublished Ed.D. thesis, University of Oregon.
Erickson, H. (1985). Conflict and the female principal. *Phi Delta Kappan*, 67(4), 288-291.
Farmer, N. (1983). *Characteristics of women principals in North Carolina*. Unpublished Ed.D. thesis, University of North Carolina, Chapel Hill.
Farrar, E., & Hampel, R. (1987). Social services in American high schools. *Phi Delta Kappan*, 69(4), 297-303.

160

Fertman, C., & Toca, O. (1989). A drug and alcohol aftercare service: Linking adolescents, families, and schools. *Journal of Alcohol and Drug Education*, 34(2), 46-53.

Forbes, D. (1987). Saying no to Ron and Nancy: School-based drug abuse prevention programs in the 1980s. *Journal of Education*, 169(3), 80-90.*

Heron, B. (1988). Eliminating drug abuse among students. *Clearing House*, 61, 215-216.

Hockman, S., & Worner, W. (1987). In-school suspension and group counseling: Helping the at-risk student. *NASSP Bulletin*, 71(501), 93-96.*

Johns, F. (1989). *School discipline guidebook.* Boston: Allyn & Bacon.*

Knoff, H. (1983). Solving school discipline problems: Look before you leap. *Clearing House*, 57, 155-157.

Lewis, J., et al. (1987). *Drug and alcohol abuse in the schools: A practical policy guide for administrators and teachers on how to combat drugs and alcohol.* ERIC, Document Number ED281304.

Lohrmann, D., & Fors, S. (1988). Can school based educational programs really be expected to solve the adolescent drug abuse problem? *Journal of Drug Education*, 18, 327-338.

Malvin, J., et al. (1985). Evaluation of two school-based alternatives programs. *Journal of Alcohol and Drug Education*, 30(3), 98-108.

Olem, R. (1988). On campus suspensions: A case study. *High School Journal*, 72(1), 36-39.*

Rosiak, J. (1987). Effective learning demands drug-free schools. *NASSP Bulletin*, 71(497), 128-133.

Rossow, L. (1989). *The law of student expulsion and suspensions.* Topeka, KS: National Organization of Legal Problems of Education.*

Sawyer, K. (1984). *The right to safe schools: A newly recognized inalienable right.* ERIC, Document Number ED253966.

Shakeshaft, C. (1989). *Women in educational administration.* Newbury Park, CA: Sage Publications.*

Shea, L. (1984). *Women and the high school principalship: A comparison of male and female aspirations and career paths.* Unpublished Ed.D. thesis, Lehigh University.

Sheppard, M. (1984). Drug abuse prevention education: What is realistic for schools? *Journal of Drug Education*, 14(4), 323-329.

Sullivan, J. (1988). *A study of the evolution of three in-school suspension programs in Virginia*. Unpublished Ed.D. thesis, College of William and Mary.

Sullivan, J. (1989). Elements of a successful in-school suspension program. *NASSP Bulletin*, 73(516), 32-38.

Washington, P. (1986). *A study of administrator and teacher perception and attitude toward inschool suspension programs at selected high schools of the metropolitan St. Louis school districts*. Unpublished Ph.D. thesis, Saint Louis University.

Watson, D., & Bright, A. (1988). So you caught them using drugs: Now what? *Thrust*, 17(3), 34-36.

Weis, L., Farrar, E., & Petrie, H. (1989). *Dropouts from schools*. Albany, NY: State University of New York Press.*

Zorn, R. (1988). New alternatives to student suspensions for substance abuse. *American Secondary Education*, 17(2), 30-32.

*readings not included in the text

CASE 23

NEVER, NEVER, NEVER TRY TO GET IN THE
TAXPAYER'S POCKET

BACKGROUND INFORMATION

There are several reasons why the literature on tax referenda provide mixed signals. Perhaps the most relevant is the nature of the community in which the action occurs. That is, what works in one school district may not work in another largely because of the attitudes, experiences, and so forth of the general population. The superintendent in this case seeks counsel from four individuals his board president, his state senator, a former boss, and a former professor. You may wish to point out to your students that it is likely that the four individuals possess varying levels of knowledge about the environment of the Eastern Boswell School District. This is a factor to consider in weighing their opinions.

When the superintendent met with the president of the teachers' association to discuss the possibility of a referendum, he added a dimension to this case. The information in the case tells us that Terry was hired in large measure to build new bridges after a bitter strike. A decision not to move forward with the referendum takes on new significance because of this consideration. It is quite likely that such a decision will have a negative effect on Terry's relationship with the teachers.

Recommending the referendum has risks. The patrons in the school district are not likely to approve such a measure (at least that is what is predicted by some individuals who are very familiar with the political environment in the community); and even if it does pass, many taxpayers will be angered by the products of victory (i.e., higher tax bills). These risks should be considered in light of financial conditions in the district. The superintendent is in a situation where a referendum appears to be his only choice to adding programs and improving employee salaries; yet, success may bring added problems.

Students who opt to step back from having a referendum should be asked: (1) how they will deal with the teachers' association, and (2) what alternatives they will pursue with regard to adding

163

programs and improving salaries. Students who move forward with the referendum should be asked: (1) how they will design the campaign to win voter approval, and (2) what plans they have to deal with disgruntled patrons.

KEY ISSUES/QUESTIONS

1. *Outline the different effects of a frozen tax rate versus a frozen tax levy. Why are the schools at a disadvantage because they have a frozen levy?* This question requires an understanding of school finance. A frozen tax rate generates more revenue as the tax base (assessed valuation) increases. A frozen levy has the effect of decreasing the tax rate as the tax base increases. In other words, under a frozen tax rate, the amount of revenue that the school district can collect from local taxes is not fixed. Under a frozen tax levy, it is. A frozen tax levy has the primary disadvantage that it does not permit a school district to benefit from economic growth in the community. School districts cannot survive very long with the same amount of annual funds, so the net effect of a frozen tax levy is an increased dependence on state funding. This is exactly what occurred in some states, such as Indiana, where tax freeze programs were put into effect.

2. *Did the superintendent do the right thing when he met with the president of the teachers' association and told her he was considering asking for a referendum?* As noted earlier, meeting with the association president added a significant dimension to this case. Strategically, the superintendent probably should not have done so unless he was absolutely sure that he was going to recommend the referendum. Some students might suggest that the superintendent needed to know if the association would support the referendum. Given that one of the intentions was to raise salaries significantly over the next two years, the superintendent could have surmised that association support was inevitable. In the final analysis, the superintendent needed to weigh the political disadvantages of conferring with the association president against the potential value of finding out if they would support the initiative.

3. *Why does the literature offer differing opinions about referenda? Should there be a set of principles that are best to follow?* You can

164

cite the following possible reasons: (a) communities differ significantly in economic, political, demographic, cultural, and social dimensions; (b) the issues in a referedum (i.e., the reasons for having one) are unique to the situation; (c) the past experiences of a community with referenda vary markedly; (d) the overall economic conditions in a country and state can have a dramatic impact; and (e) campaign strategies are often the product of philosophical objective considerations.

4. *Why do so many taxpayers and elected officials believe that schools are inefficient organizations?* The average taxpayer is prone to use the same ruler to measure productivity in a school system as is used to measure profit in a corporation. Many patrons maintain a narrow view of what the school should accomplish (usually restricted to teaching the basics), but they also are quick to criticize schools when social problems plague society (e.g., drugs, crime, teenage pregnancies). School officials have not done a very good job of explaining that success in public education is not measured solely by per pupil costs or by test score outcomes. Students in your class should be encouraged to explore ways that they can communicate that each school district is unique and deserves to be judged in the context of its specific mission, needs, and so forth.

5. *Is Superintendent Severta looking in the right place for information? Would you have looked elsewhere for information and advice?* With the possible exception of his meeting with the association president, it is difficult to criticize the superintendent's effort to gain information. Other possibilities for seeking information and advice include the following: (1) state and national associations (e.g., state administrator groups, state school board association); (2) superintendents who have been through referenda in the same state recently; (3) meetings with influential figures in the community (e.g., bankers, large property owners); (4) consultants who specialize in this area (e.g., political analysts, economists).

6. *If you were the superintendent, would you believe the board president when he says he will do what he can to get the other four board members to approve the referendum?* There is nothing in the case that leads students to believe that the board president is insincere in making this statement. If students respond that they do not trust him, you should pursue the reasons prompting this answer. At

165

times, students who take this position will express a general mistrust of school board members or of the entire process of public decision making (i.e., they believe you should never be too confident of anyone keeping their word in a highly political situation). Keep in mind that the board president has not promised to support the referendum itself. Differences in student backgrounds and experiences should be illuminated if they indeed lead to varying responses to this question.

7. *How do you interpret Senator Tiles's comments that "the referendum was never intended to be a viable alternative for raising additional funds?"* Essentially what the senator is saying that no one should be surprised that most referenda fail. If the legislator wanted to create an effective alternative for raising local taxes, they would have designed the process differently. The option was provided to allow some atypical communities to raise taxes if they wished. The senator assumes that the vast majority of taxpayers are not inclined to vote to raise taxes for schools.

8. *React to the advice that Terry received from his former boss. Is he right? What leads you to agree or disagree with this advice?* Superintendents confront a number of issues that divide communities. Tax increases are among the most volatile. The warning that taxpayers never forget if you raise their rates is an overstatement. You should advise your students to be wary of such sweeping generalizations. Affluent suburbs, for instance, often react to referenda much differently than rural communities. If the advice is considered within the specific context of this case (i.e., within the environment of the school district described), it may be of value. As a warning for all school districts, it is less valid.

9. *Is it common for superintendents to face situations where political and professional considerations are in conflict? Is this more or less true in other professions (e.g., law, medicine)?* Most physicians and lawyers operate in the private sector of the economy, thus they are less likely to be faced with these choices. In large measure, the condition faced by superintendents relates to their working in the public sector rather than the specific nature of their professional responsibilities. City managers and other governmental employees often face the same difficult choices that confront school superintendents. Expanded or improved services may require voter approval.

166

OTHER SUGGESTED ACTIVITIES

1. Have your students identify the school finance conditions in your state related to: (1) referenda; (2) the division between state and local support for education; (3) the provisions for tax levies and tax rates; (4) restrictions on increasing local taxes.

2. Invite two superintendents to your class who have recently been through referenda. One should be from a district where the initiative passed and one from a district where it failed. Have them discuss the differences and to comment on this case.

3. Invite a political science professor to your class to discuss the case.

SUGGESTED READINGS:

Banicki, G. (1987). *The study of potential voter behavior to an educational tax referendum.* Unpublished Ed.D. thesis, Northern Illinois University.

Black, J., & English, F. (1986). *What they don't tell you in schools of education about school administration*, chap. 16. Lancaster, PA: Technomic.

Chopra, R. (1988). How we passed a bond issue hard on the heels of a tax hike. *American School Board Journal*, 176(6), 26, 29.

Clodi, D. (1987). *The relationship between educational tax rate referendum outcome and both campaign strategies and selected demographic variables.* Unpublished Ed.D. thesis, Illinois State University.

Dana, J. (1985). *A field study of voter behavior in school bond election failures.* Unpublished Ph.D. thesis, University of Missouri, Columbia.

First, P. (1986). Here's how press coverage can boost (or bust) your next school referendum. *American School Board Journal*, 173(11), 42.

Goldstein, W. (1984). *Selling school budgets in hard times*, Fastback 215. Bloomington, IN: Phi Delta Kappa Educational Foundation.*

Guthrie, J., Garms, W., & Pierce, L. (1988). *School finance and public policy* (2nd ed.), chap. 5. Englewood Cliffs, NJ: Prentice-Hall.

167

Hahn, H., & Kamieniecki, S. (1987). *Referendum voting,* pp. 119-131. Westport, CT: Greenwood Press.

Hamel, G. (1984). Fairfax county loves its schools. *School Business Affairs,* 50(2), 32, 50.

Henry, J. (1987). Help for passing bond referenda. *School Business Affairs,* 53(12), 26-27.

Humphrey, S., & Weber, J. (1985). Why finance elections fail: Passive referendum campaigns are no longer effective. *Journal of Educational Public Relations,* 8(3), 30-33.

Kaiser, H., & Nelson, G. (1982). Inequality and the Minnesota referendum levy. *Journal of Education Finance,* 8(2), 152-169.

Ornstein, A. (1989). Trimming the fat, stretching the meat for the 1990s budgets. *The School Administrator,* 9(46), 20-21.

Ross, V. (1983). Don't be daunted by defeat: Score a bond issue victory. *Executive Educator,* 5(4), 25-26.

Walker, B. (1984). The local property tax for public schools: Some historical perspectives. *Journal of Education Finance,* 9(3), 265-288.

*readings not included in the text

CASE 24

THE CLINIC CONTROVERSY

BACKGROUND INFORMATION

The growing number of teenage pregnancies and related health concerns for sexually active high school students (e.g., AIDS) have largely been responsible for the creation of school health clinics in the United States. Such clinics have emerged in urban areas where a significant number of students either do not have parents or have parents who are incapable of providing direction and assistance.

This case exemplifies a political/professional dilemma for the superintendent. In this respect, it is similar to Case 23. On the one hand, the superintendent has a responsibility to lead. He is the professional who gives direction to a lay school board. On the other hand, does it do anyone any good to put forward a recommendation that appears to be doomed to failure? Typically, students in your class will disagree on the course of action. Some will embrace an idealistic posture indicating that ethical/moral convictions lead them to make a specific recommendation. Others will adopt a pragmatic view based largely on political considerations. These individuals are more apt to focus on the long term effects of a defeated recommendation on their careers.

One question you should pursue relates to how a withdrawal of the recommendation will be viewed by the administrators and teachers in the school district. Will they interpret withdrawal as a sign of weakness? Although this alternative appears to be a better political decision, students should not conclude that withdrawing the recommendation will eradicate political problems.

KEY ISSUES/QUESTIONS

1. *Relate the community to this problem. Does the nature of the community have any special influence on this case?* Students may immediately draw some assumptions from demographic information supplied in the case. For instance, the large Italian-American population in Shelton may be seen by some as a large Catholic

169

population. Furthermore, this perception may lead to conclusions about the mounting opposition to the idea of health clinics. As in all school/community interactions, the community environment is important. A program that works well in one setting may or may not work equally well in another. In this vein, it is interesting to note that the two clinics visited by Shelton officials were both in large, urban systems. The populations in these areas may have been more homogeneous than in Shelton. The cultural diversity of Shelton makes differing views on topics such as birth control and abortion very likely.

2. *Identify the issues that make student health clinics controversial.* The issues that make the health clinic controversial are those that tend to divide many Americans--namely, abortion, birth control, and sex education. Far fewer citizens object to interventions aimed at drug abuse. When moral and religious dimensions enter the picture, the conflict is almost always intensified. Many political scientists have noted that abortion has been the most divisive issue in America since the Civil War.

3. *Evaluate the procedures employed by Dr. Ochman in reaching his recommendation in this matter. Do you believe he was influenced by his own values and beliefs?* Dr. Ochman tries to have varying segments of the community represented in studying the problems associated with drop-outs and teenage pregnancies. The creation of the study committee and the subsequent discussions with community leaders are positive actions. The case does not reveal if suggestions other than health clinics were presented to the superintendent. We learn that there were differences of opinion among community leaders regarding potential solutions. You may want to ask students if it would have been a good idea for the superintendent to engage the community leaders in a long-term study focusing specifically on health clinics in high schools. Students may disagree as to whether the superintendent is influenced by his own values and beliefs. This condition is analogous to elected officials taking a position on legalized abortion. When you disagree with the officials, you tend to believe they are not capable of being objective.

4. *Identify the advantages and disadvantages of the superintendent: (a) insisting that his recommendation be acted on at the July board meeting, and (b) withdrawing his recommendation in order to spare*

170

the board the necessity of voting on the matter. By insisting on a vote, the superintendent could say he was performing his responsibility to put forward what he believed to be the best recommendation. If the motion is defeated, the board members voting against the recommendation will be blamed by the supporters of the concept. By forcing the vote, the superintendent may anger some board members who would prefer not to have to take a public stand on this issue. Withdrawing the motion is likely to relieve those board members opposed to the program. They may view the superintendent in a favorable light. Given the circumstances presented in the case, the superintendent should be prepared to give an explanation if he withdraws his recommendation (i.e., because he already made it once during the June board meeting). Simply stating that he knew his recommendation could not be approved will not suffice with many professional staff members and citizens. One possibility would be for the superintendent to withdraw the motion, indicating that he will continue to work with community leaders to find possible solutions that may be more palatable for the board and community.

5. *Are data concerning the relationship between pregnancies and drop-out rates in Shelton typical for the United States? What are the figures in your school district?* The figures presented in this case are indicative of the nation as a whole. Statistics presented in the case (e.g., relationship between poverty and pregnancies; relationship between pregnancy and drop-out rates) come from national studies. Most educators are not able to immediately identify these statistics for their own place of employment and/or community. Doing so makes a good assignment for your students.

6. *How much emphasis would you place on the information collected when the two school officials visited health clinics in other cities?* The information in the case suggests that the two clinics existed in somewhat different environments. If they were inner-city schools, for example, the populations may be substantially different from the school in this case. Parental objections to school health clinics may be related not only to religion and culture, but also to economic and social factors as well.

7. *Should board members have stated their position on this matter prior to a formal vote being taken?* It is widely accepted that the

authority of board members is restricted to collective action. That is, their vote only matters when an official vote is taken. More practically, however, it is somewhat unrealistic to believe that individuals on school boards will refuse to state personal beliefs and convictions on controversial issues. In many instances, stating views prior to an official vote constitutes a political strategy. The board member may want the other board members to know how the public reacts to the controversy. By stating an early position, the board member puts the issue before the public. Elected congressmen and senators frequently use this tactic to test political support and/or to build momentum for their position. The critical question is not whether it is right or wrong to state positions before an official vote, but rather how the superintendent should deal with such situations when they occur.

8. *Should a superintendent withdraw recommendations when it is obvious that there is no chance they will be approved?* As noted earlier, this case presents a conflict between what many will see as a professional responsibility (to make a recommendation) and a political consideration (possibly alienating a majority of the board and a good portion of the community). Withdrawal of the recommendation appropriately should be considered in the context of the reasons that spawn this action. If, for example, the withdrawal is motivated by a desire for further study and compromise, it will be judged differently than if it is simply the product of political fears. There is no simple answer to this question. You should discuss the organizational and community variables that need to be weighed by the superintendent (e.g., community values, religious beliefs, faculty support).

9. *Do you think that linkages with community agencies are a good idea? Why or why not?* Increasingly, community agencies are seeking ways of building bridges. This action is generated by dwindling resources and an ever increasing demand for services. School officials recognize that many problems cannot be resolved by any single agency. This is true because troubled students frequently need physical, psychological and social interventions to improve educational performance. Thus, the concept of agency linkage is growing in popularity.

OTHER SUGGESTED ACTIVITIES

1. Invite several community leaders to your class to discuss this issue. Try to get persons who represent opposing views.

2. Generate a discussion of the responsibility of public schools to deal with issues such as sex education, AIDS, and teenage pregnancies.

3. Communicating directly with a principal in a school where such a clinic exists can be very beneficial. If such a person is not able to meet directly with your class, you may want to consider a conference telephone call or a teleconference.

4. Invite a professor from one of the behavioral sciences to your class to discuss why issues involving religious beliefs tend to have such a divisive effect on citizens.

SUGGESTED READINGS:

Barth, R. (1989). *Reducing the risk Building skills to reduce teen pregnancies*. Santa Cruz, CA: Network Publishing.*

Berger, M. (1982). The public schools can't do it all. *Contemporary Education*, 54(1), 6-8.

Bowers, L. (1985). *Religion and education: A study of the interrelationship between fundamentalism and education in contemporary America*. Unpublished Ed.D. thesis, East Tennessee State University.

Buie, J. (1987). Schools must act on teen pregnancy. *The School Administrator*, 44(8), 12-15.

Buie, J. (1987). Teen pregnancy It's time for schools to tackle the problem. *Phi Delta Kappan*, 68(10), 737-739.

Cook, L. (1987). This proposed health clinic triggered a rhetorical meltdown. *American School Board Journal*, 174(5), 27-28.

Cuban, L. (1988). A fundamental puzzle of school reform. *Phi Delta Kappan*, 70(5), 341-344.

Edwards, L., & Brent, N. (1987). Grapple with those tough issues before giving that clinic the go ahead. *American School Board Journal*, 174(5), 25-27.

Ennis, T. (1987). Prevention of pregnancy among adolescents: Part I, the school's role. *School Law Bulletin,* 18(2), 1-15.

Frymier, J., & Gansneder, B. (1989). The Phi Delta Kappa study of published between 1978 and 1986).

Gilloti, P. (1988). *Teenage pregnancy: A research guide for programs and services.* Buffalo, NY: W. S. Hein.*

Hahn, A. (1987). Reaching out to America's dropouts: What to do? *Phi Delta Kappan,* 69(4), 256-263.

Kirby, D., & Lovick, S. (1987). School-based health clinics. *Educational Horizons,* 65,(3), 139-143.

Ladner, J. (1987). Black teenage pregnancy: A challenge for educators. (Special issue: The Black child's home environment and student achievement.) *Journal of Negro Educationed,* 56(1), 53-63.*

McClellan, M. (Ed.) (1987). School based clinics and other controversial issues in education. Westchester, IL: Crossway Books.*

Miller, D. (1990). *The case for school-based health clinics,* Fastback 300. Bloomington, IN: Phi Delta Kappa Foundation.*

Mossbacker, B. (Ed.) (1987). School based clinics and other controversial issues in education. Westchester, IL: Crossway Books.*

Norris, B. (1985). High school pregnancy clinic survives storm. *Times Educational Supplement,* 3617 (October 25), 17.

Peng, S. (1987). Effective high schools: What are the attributes? In J. Land & H. Waldberg (Eds.), *Effective school leadership,* pp. 89-108. Berkeley, CA: McCutcheon.

Ravitch, D. (1982). The new right and the schools: Why mainstream America is listening to our critics. *American Teacher,* 6(3), 8-13, 46.

Schwartz, D., & Darabi, K. (1986). Motivations for adolescents' first visit to a family planning clinic. *Adolescents,* 21, 535-545.

Will, S., & Brown, L. (1988). School-based health clinics: What role? *American Teacher,* 72(3), 4.

*readings not included in the text

CASE 25

A MATTER OF HONOR

BACKGROUND INFORMATION

Students in educational administration are exposed to a number of readings that concentrate on the relationship between public institutions and the society in which they exist. This case presents a community environment with several distinctive characteristics:

1. Newton is a heterogeneous community. The residents exhibit a variety of values and beliefs, because of the cultural, ethnic, and racial diversity.

2. A common experience for many residents in the community has been the labor union. To some extent, the union constituted a unifying force. As the union diminishes in influence, the philosophy of this organization has less effect on community life.

3. The community has moved rather rapidly from a condition of munificence to a condition of scarcity. That is, the economy once flourished and resources were available for development. Industrial retrenchment has created an opposite trend in the past decade.

Additionally there are other features of the school district that are noteworthy:

1. Most administrators were promoted within the organization (as opposed to employing administrators from outside of the school district).

2. The athletic successes of the high school were a source of community pride.

3. The employees of the school district are unionized and somewhat aggressive as evidenced by recent strikes.

175

4. The school board members seem to represent the diversity of the community as a whole.

THE CHALLENGE

When students are placed in the position of Mr. Furtoski, they should be directed to respond from the perspective of their own education and experiences. This permits students to personalize the response. That is, it allows students to answer the question as if they were truly the principal in this situation. Students should not be allowed to alter other conditions in the case (e.g., the climate of the school district, the nature of the community).

Certainly how a student responds to this challenge is important. What is even more important, however, is the rationale students are able to articulate for the choice they make. It is especially cogent that students are able to relate their behavior to professional knowledge or personal experiences. Consider the following examples:

1. Deciding to compromise. The student defends this alternative on the grounds of the nature of the school district and the community. Unionism and collective bargaining are heavily skewed toward shared decisions and compromise. Or the student defends this choice by arguing that the welfare of the entire community must be considered in reaching a decision.

2. Deciding not to compromise. Students may defend this position by noting that it is a matter of ethics. Or students may contend that the principal has a responsibility to defend the decision of the teacher. Or students may advance the notion that accepting compromise will only generate greater conflict--this time with the teachers' union. Another possibility would be for students to defend this behavior by contending that administrators only administer policy and if the board wanted to compromise, they should change their own policy on plagiarism.

1. *Identify the possible alternatives that the principal may pursue in this matter. Evaluate the merits of each.* Some students may quickly judge that the principal has only two choices in this matter: (1) accept the compromise or (2) reject the compromise. Actually, he has a much wider range of alternatives. Consider the following:

> 1. The principal could ask for several days to study the matter more fully. This would allow him additional time to weigh the advantages and disadvantages more carefully.
> 2. He could tell the board that he does not want to respond until he has had a chance to confer with both the teacher and the superintendent. He then could pass the problem directly to the superintendent by indicating that he will go along with any decision Mr. Sposis makes.
> 3. He could indicate that he will do whatever the school board thinks is best.
> 4. He could try to place the pressure on the teacher (and the teachers' union) by indicating that he is willing to compromise but that the teacher is not so inclined. In pursuing this path, the principal warns the board that union problems are likely if the board does not stand behind the teacher.
> 5. The principal could respond by saying that it is not his responsibility to make recommendations to the school board.
> 6. He could attempt to pass the problem directly to the school board's attorney by responding that the issue is essentially a legal matter and that the board should follow the attorney's advice.

Having students analyze the advantages and disadvantages of each of these responses is a valuable experience. It is especially important that students be able to express insights into the ways that personal philosophy, organizational climate, and the community environment contribute to any of these choices.

2. *Do you think the teacher could have been more flexible in this matter?* Individuals differ markedly in their beliefs about policy. Some students may respond that the teacher has no choice but to follow school board policy. Others may take a view that the teacher should be compassionate and allow the student to have another chance. You can point out how the individual teacher is a key

variable in this case. Another teacher may have looked the other way.

3. *To what extent do you think the economic environment of the school district (the community) affects this situation?* Some aspects of organizational theory are very important to this question. For example, work on munificence and scarcity of environmental resources is enlightening. As this community struggles to revive its economic vitality, citizens may expect (or demand) that the public institutions take risks, alter standard behaviors, and the like.

4. *Is the fact that Newton is a "union" town important to this case? Would the situation be any different if it occurred in a wealthy suburb of Detroit?* The very nature of labor unions produces a set of values and beliefs about decision making, conflict, and compromise that are in sharp contrast to the tenets of bureaucracy. Members of unions are far less likely to blindly accept the legitimate authority of school district officials. By contrast, wealthy suburban areas are often occupied by "corporate types"--executives who believe that authority within organizations must be respected. A principal should take note of the fact that the decision in this matter will be weighed by the general public in the context of their prevailing values and beliefs.

5. *Most of the administrators in Newton acquired their positions via internal promotions. Do you think this has any bearing on this case?* Using internal promotions may be one indicator that the school board and superintendent are influenced by unionism. That is, unions frequently advance internal promotions as a means of creating organizational loyalty. A useful exercise related to this question is to ask students to compare a school district in an affluent area of your state with another district that is essentially "blue collar." Have them investigate if the promotion policies or practices differ in these school systems. In some parts of the country, citizens view jobs in public education to be quasi patronage positions.

6. *Was the principal correct in immediately deciding to side with the teacher in this matter when he contacted the superintendent? What, if anything, would you have done differently after first learning about the charges of plagiarism?* Often administrators act quickly without properly weighing alternative behaviors. The fact that the

178

principal immediately decided that the teacher's position was the correct position could be criticized. Graduate students are repeatedly told that they should develop and assess contingencies before acting (unless time absolutely does not permit). Siding with the teacher was the safe thing to do. However, the principal did nothing to resolve the problem at his level.

7. *To what extent would your decision on whether to accept the parent's proposal be predicated on the fact that the board is divided on this issue?* As noted earlier, individuals exhibit substantial behavioral differences. Leaders are no exception. Students may differ in their sensitivity to political issues. Some students may view the division on the board as a very significant matter. Others may be idealists, arguing that the leader's responsibility is to be ethical, to follow policy, to not compromise, and so forth.

8. *Can you think of any possible solutions other than the one proposed by the parents?* It could be argued that accepting the parents' offer to settle this matter is not a compromise but rather outright accommodation. The following are some other possible solutions:

    a. Allow the student to take the class over but stipulate that she must do so with the same teacher.
    b. Have the board change its policy.
    c. Have the board formally grant an exception to their own policy based on the outstanding record of this student.
    d. Allow the student to take the course at another high school (or local college).
    e. Allow the student to drop the class without a grade and permit her to enroll in a substitute course.

The focal point of having students respond to this question should be the realization that many alternatives usually exist for problems. Only through identifying cogent alternatives and interfacing them with environmental and organizational conditions can the principal respond in an educated fashion.

9. *If you were the superintendent, how would you react in this matter?* In this case, the school board places the pressure directly on the principal. Some students may contend that the superintendent has a responsibility to intervene. He should protect Mr. Furtoski and not allow the board to demand a decision directly from the principal.

Others may decide that the superintendent should have alerted the principal to what the board would want and that the principal and superintendent should have been prepared to give the board a unified response. Still other students criticize the principal for not resolving the conflict at the building level.

10. *Should growing community tensions play any part in this decision? Why or why not?* Racial tensions are important to this case. Students are apt to exhibit significant differences with regard to emphasizing the needs of the community versus the needs of the organization. In other words, some students will focus on the organization. They will argue that policies and rules must be protected. Students who exhibit a sensitivity for the environment may believe that the community needs should come first. These students are more apt to consider accepting the offer made by the parents or countering with another position designed to achieve compromise. Ask your students to identify ways of making the school board aware of the needs of both the school district and community.

OTHER SUGGESTED ACTIVITIES

1. Invite a leader of organized labor and/or a corporate executive to class. See how this person would react to this case.

2. Have students examine legal definitions of plagiarism and see if they can identify cases in school law that involved disciplinary actions against students who were found guilty of plagiarism.

3. Discuss in detail the role of the superintendent in this matter. In particular, develop alternative strategies that the superintendent could have employed.

SUGGESTED READINGS:

Alexander, J. (1988). The ethics of borrowing. *College Teaching*, 36(1), 21-24.*
Brooks, G. (1989). Exploring plagiarism in the composition classroom. *Freshman English News*, 17(2), 31-35.

Browlee, G. (1987). Coping with plagiarism requires several strategies. *Journalism Educator,* 41(4), 25-29.

Clark, I. (1988). Collaboration and ethics in writing center pedagogy. *Writing Center Journal,* 9(1), 3-12.*

Curry, J. (1987). The instructional writing assignment: Making it work. *Bulletin of the Association for Business Communication,* 50(3), 29-30.*

Dant, D. (1986). Plagiarism in high school: A survey. *English Journal,* 75(2), 81-84.

Drum, A. (1986). Responding to plagiarism. *College Composition and Communication,* 37(2), 241-243.

Fass, R. (1986). By honor bound: Encouraging academic honesty. *Educational Record,* 67(4), 32-36.

Gathercoal, F. (1987). *Judicious discipline.* Ann Arbor, MI: Prakken Publishing.*

Geosits, M., & Kirk, W. (1983). Sowing the seeds of plagiarism. *Principal,* 62(5), 35-38.

Jackson, L., et al. (1987). Dear teacher, Johnny copied. *Reading Teacher,* 41(1), 22-25.

Kibler, W., et al. (1988). *Academic integrity and student development: Legal issues and policy perspectives.* Asheville, NC: College Administration Publications.*

Kroll, B. (1988). How college freshmen view plagiarism. *Written communication,* 5(2), 204-221.*

Martin, B. (1984). Plagiarism and responsibility. *Journal of Tertiary Educational Administration,* 6(2), 183-190.

Mawdsley, R. (1985). *Legal aspects of plagiarism.* Topeka, KS: National Organization on Legal Problems of Education.*

Peterson, P. (1984). Plagiarism: It can happen to you. *Quill and Scroll,* 58(4), 15.

Roberts, R. (1986). Public university responses to academic dishonesty: Disciplinary or academic. *Journal of Law and Education,* 15(4), 369-384.*

Sauer, R. (1983). Coping with copiers. *English Journal,* 72(4), 50-52.

Shea, J. (1987). When borrowing becomes burglary. *Currents,* 13(1), 38-42.

Singhal, A. (1983). How to halt student dishonesty. *College Student Journal,* 17(1), 13-19.*

Skom, E. (1986). Plagiarism: Quite a rather bad little crime. *AAHE Bulletin,* (October 3), 7.

* readings not included in text

READING LIST FOR CASE METHOD
(These readings may be helpful if you wish to explore the
foundations of the case study method in greater depth.)

Baxter, V. (1988). A case-study method for teaching industrial
  sociology. *Teaching Sociology,* 16(1), 21-24.
Christensen, C. (1987). *Teaching and the case method: Text, cases,
  and readings.* Boston: Harvard Business School.
Clark, V. (1986). The effectiveness of case studies in training
  principals, using the deliberative orientation. *Peabody Journal
  of Education,* 63, 187-195.
Erskine, J., Leenders, M., & Maufette-Leenders (1981). *Teaching
  with cases.* London, Ontario: University of Western Ontario.
Garsombke, D., & Garsombke, T. (1987). *Strategic case analysis: A
  systematic approach for students in business and management.*
  Dubuque, IA: Kendall/Hunt.
Henson, K. (1988). Case study in teacher education. *Educational
  Forum,* 52, 235-241.
Kowalski, T. (1990). The case method and situational learning.
  Journal of Human Behavior and Learning, 2(7).
Kowalski, T., Weaver, R., & Henson, K. (1990). *Case studies on
  teaching: Instructor's guide.* New York: Longman.
Lovelock, C. (1986). Teaching with cases. *New Directions for
  Continuing Education,* 25, 30, 35.
Masoner, M. (1988). *An audit of the case method.* New York:
  Praeger.
Neustadt, R., & May, E. (1986). *Thinking in time: The uses of
  history for decision-makers.* New York: Free Press.
Romm, T., & Mahler, S. (1986). A three dimensional model for
  using case studies in the academic classroom. *Higher
  Education,* 15(6), 677-696.
Ronstadt, R. (1980). *The art of case analysis: A guide to the
  diagnosis of business situations.* Dover, MA: Lord Publishing.
Schon, D. (1990). *Educating the reflective practitioner.* San
  Francisco: Jossey-Bass.
Schroeder, H. (1984). Peer evaluation in case analysis. *Journal of
  Business Education,* 60, 73-77.
Scully, A. (1984). The case method. *History and Social Science
  Teacher,* 19(3), 178-180.

Towl, A. (1969). *To study administration by cases.* Boston: Harvard University, Graduate School of Business Administration.

Welty, W. (1989). Discussion method teaching: How to make it work. *Change,* 21(4), 40-49.